CRYSTALS

CROSSES

AND

CHAKRAS

CRYSTALS CROSSES
AND
CHAKRAS

A WOMAN'S
MYSTICAL EMERGENCE

WILMA WAKE

Chrysalis Books
West Chester, Pennsylvania

Library of Congress Cataloging-in-Publication Data

Wake, Wilma
    Crystals, crosses, and chakras: a woman's mystical emergence / Wilma Wake.
        p.   cm.
    Includes bibliographic references
    ISBN 0-87785-391-6 (pbk.)
    1. Wake, Wilma   2. Swedenborgians—United States—Biography.
    I. Title.
BX8749.W35 A3 2000
289'.4'092—dc21   99–087536
[B]

Edited by Patte LeVan; additional editing by Mary Lou Bertucci
Cover design by Caroline Kline, based on original art by Rob Schouten
Interior design by Sans Serif, Inc.
Set in Goudy by Sans Serif, Inc., Saline, Michigan

Art Credit: Cover background image by Rob Schouten, copyright 1996, used by permission of the artist.

Printed in the United States of America.

Chrysalis Books is an imprint of the Swedenborg Foundation Publishers. For more information, contact:

    Chrysalis Books
    Swedenborg Foundation Publishers
    320 N. Church Street
    West Chester, Pennsylvania 19380
    (610) 430-3222
        Or
    http://www.swedenborg.com

CONTENTS

PART 3
CHAKRAS: 1995–PRESENT

INTRODUCTION

It is a gorgeous fall day today, as I sit in the backyard of my little house in rural New Hampshire. As usual, my four feline companions are curled about me as I write.

It was twenty years ago, in the fall of 1979, that I first became a published author in a step that altered my life forever. I wrote about my spiritual journey in which I had experienced a psychic awakening and found support in New Age communities. I was terrified to have my story made public, and I asked to be published under a pseudonym.

Even with a different name, however, I could not hide, and I found myself speaking to many others—publicly and privately—about my spiritual journey.

What I did not realize then, and had to learn the hard way, is that I was in the very early stages of the spiritual path. I had encountered exciting psychic experiences, but had yet to walk the mystical path common to many religious traditions. I had yet to walk through a dark night of the soul, to experience mystical love towards God, and to seek union with my Beloved.

My first book, *Beyond the Body*, was published in 1979, and a sequel followed in 1981. *Beyond the Body* was then re-issued in 1985. At that time, I made the decision to issue the book under my real name. I was then in a Christian seminary, feeling a call to ordained ministry. As I publicly claimed my psychic journey, I was confronted with many questions about how I could expect to combine the psychic with Christian ministry. I didn't have many answers. And I was shattered that the publication of my story under my real name seemed to play a major role in my ordination's being put on hold indefinitely. I became angry at God, distanced myself from my spirituality, and vowed that I would never again publish any account of my spiritual experiences.

That was before I found God back in my life in a new way. I discovered a mystical mentor of the past in the writings of Emanuel Swedenborg and found a new affirmation and understanding of my spirituality. I was thrilled to learn that Swedenborg's writings were the central part of a small denomination, the Swedenborgian Church. I attended the Swedenborg School of Religion in Newton, Massachusetts, and became ordained as a Swedenborgian minister in 1990. I felt secure in having a church community to which I was accountable, and a theological framework in which to explore my spiritual life. It was then that my mystical life took off with renewed vigor, and I found myself walking a mystical path that so many have done throughout history.

I discovered that psychic phenomena is not, in itself, the path and, in fact, can hinder one on the path. It is often part of the path, and the many mystical traditions guide one into integrating its experiences into a larger spirituality. I learned how Emanuel Swedenborg had done that in his life and his writings.

As I allowed my spirituality to emerge, I encountered the romantic, blissful love of longing for the Lord and the ecstasy that comes from the closeness in that relationship. Yet, I also discovered that the Beloved did not love my ego as I did, but rather sought to diminish its strength. I encountered the harsh demands of the Beloved and realized that I had to take my spiritual experiences into the world where they could be tested and shaped. As part of that process, I again felt a call to write about my spiritual journey.

My ego greatly rebelled at first, remembering all that had ensued after I last published. But over time, the Beloved taught me to spend less time in my ego state and more time with the part of my self that is in union with the Divine. At first I wrote out of obedience, but then did so in joy as my struggles with God melted into partnership.

I came to realize that to hold to personal fears was to continue living in the earthbound ego. In fact, I came to appreciate many reasons for writing again. One is to complete the story I began twenty years ago. I still accept the reality of those psychic experiences, but I now see them in context. I realize the dangers inherent in them had I refused to grow beyond them. I see that the path we are all called to is one of spiritual growth. Psychic experiences may or may not be part of that path. The psychic is optional; spirituality is not. I had to move beyond my fascination with the psychic before I found the deeper spiritual truths that I believe are in all mystical traditions.

Another reason I came to accept writing again is the loneliness I have felt on this journey. My reticence to talk about my spirituality is not just personal; I believe it is cultural. I think that as a culture we need to be more open with each other and share our stories. I had to peruse the shelves of many libraries to find the stories or biographies of mystics that helped me understand my own experiences. I realized that I had much in common with the seekers of the past, although my own story was tinged with the perceptions of modern times. Although the Divine remains the same, my story reflects the culture in which I live, one of childhood abuse, marriage and divorce, eating disorders, and the struggle to understand what it means to be a woman minister today. It is a journey that expands the New Age, Christianity, and Eastern spiritualities.

New Age spirituality gave me the support I needed to start this journey. Christian mysticism gave me the context and pathway to move beyond the psychic. The Sufis helped me understand the Beloved. The yoga traditions from the Hindus helped me recognize the role of chakras and energies on my journey. Throughout, I have found my mentor, Emanuel Swedenborg, to help me move in and out of traditions, weaving them all together in one mystical emergence.

I write this book because I think that mysticism is more common today than ever before. In our technological age, we communicate and learn more than ever and have the benefit of exploring many traditions. All of this, I believe, has opened us to an age of spiritual exploration never seen before. The path today is the same as it always has been, yet it is marked anew by each generation. I felt a need to share a story that is both traditional and modern as a way of encouraging more modern stories to be shared so that we can open a dialogue with each other.

When I published twenty years ago, I was of two minds: I felt that I had either reached an end-point of spiritual development or was going crazy. Today, I know that neither is true. My mystical life has been tested for so many years in my work as a social worker, minister, and seminary faculty member that I have come to accept it as normal and healthy. I also have found deep humility, realizing how little of the path I have trod, how much yet lies ahead, and how easy it is for the human ego to take over at any time. I have come to realize that this path cannot be walked alone, but must be trodden in community with others. I have sought out communities to support and challenge my spirituality. The most important ones to me are the Swedenborgian Church, the Sisters of Mercy in New Hampshire (Region II), and the Golden Sufis in the United States.

Now, I take my story to a larger community. I invite all readers of this material into sharing our own stories and exchanging ideas on how the Divine is present in our world today. Please read this small book as I have written it: not as the end of a story, but the beginning of a relationship and the opening of a dialogue.

I am grateful for the help of many people who gave me feedback and suggestions on my manuscript. They include my superb editors Patte LeVan and Mary Lou Bertucci, as well as many other people generous with their time, including: the Reverend Eric Allison; Dot Cormier, R.S.M.; M. Alice Cassidy, R.S.M.; the Reverend Nadine Cotton; Dr. David Eller; Janet Esposito Daigle, LICSW; the Reverend Dr. George Dole; Edwina Gateley; the Reverend Emily Geohegan; the Reverend Dr. Dorothea Harvey; Johanna Hedbor; the Reverend Dr. Anne Ierardi; Dr. Robert Johnson; the Reverend Dr. Robert Kirven; Dr. Mary Kay Klein; the Reverend Dr. Ted Klein; the Reverend Jim Lassen-Willems; Kate McGinnity; Scott Ormsbee; Gayle Pershouse; Barbara-Joyce Reed, M.Ed.; the Reverend Laurie Rofinot; Dr. Alice B. Skinner; Virginia Slayton; Dr. Stuart Sovatsky; Leith Speiden; the Reverend Leanne Tigert; Dr. Llewellyn Vaughan-Lee; Bob Wake; and the Reverend Gladys Wheaton.

I am humbly grateful for so much help. Yet, I take responsibility for the final statements and conclusions I reach.

Wilma Wake
W. Franklin, New Hampshire

PROLOGUE
JUNE 29, 1994

Today, I am in the auditorium of Marymount College in Washington, D.C. I am here to celebrate the Friday morning memorial communion service at the annual convocation of the Convention branch of the Swedenborgian Church. The music is beginning, and people are arriving. Someone puts a cup of coffee in my hand. I sip it, preoccupied, as I peek through the auditorium's stage door at the gathering crowd. I am always nervous at this moment before a communion service. There are so many details to remember; it's like being in a play with memorized lines and gestures. I've been an ordained minister for only a few years, and this is the first communion I've given at our annual convention. I feel new and awkward, worried about making a stupid mistake in front of a hundred people who know me.

I'm glad that I'm not alone, but am assisting another minister. I smile at Eric. He looks a little nervous, too, as he gulps down his coffee.

The taped music starts playing, and Eric signals me to begin. I put down my cup and follow my co-celebrant to the altar that we created on the auditorium stage. I should be focused on God, but I am thinking about what I must say and do.

It's time now. I am to consecrate the bread; then Eric will consecrate the wine. I've memorized the words: "When it was evening, Jesus sat at the table with the twelve disciples; and as they were eating, he took bread, and blessed, and broke it, and gave it to them and said, 'Take, eat, this is my body.'" I break the bread. Now Eric is saying something . . . something about the cup. He is serving me communion, and I am serving him.

Now I am stepping down from the stage holding the silver plate with the broken bread—I can't seem to remember what I am doing. Now I am standing in front of a line of people moving towards me. A woman approaches with hands cupped and open. I realize I am putting a piece of bread in her hands, saying "the body of Christ; the bread of heaven."

But I don't remember why I am saying those words. I don't remember being an "I." There is only Love, and it is flowing through me, through the bread, through each person in the room. We are aglow with a divine light. The auditorium is pulsating with ecstatic energy—God is here! We are part of God. Everything is part of God. God is Love, pure Love. There is nothing else and never needs to be anything else. So simple—it's just Love.

Did a moment pass? Or an eternity? I hear music still playing. I see the end of the line of people walking up to receive communion bread from me. Have I been serving communion? Is there an "I"? Then I hear an inner voice.

We are joined together now, in a state of union.
I have been preparing you for this for a long

time. And you have resisted. But now you have dropped the barrier, and our merging is forever.

Somewhere inside I find a part that still remembers being an "I." That part responds to the inner voice:

What's happening? I don't understand! I didn't choose this.

Would you want to choose it to end?

Oh, no! Not ever! I don't care how this happened or why. I don't care what I had to go through to get here. I didn't realize before that this is the goal of life. Oneness with this Love is all that matters. You truly are Love Divine, and I want nothing else than to be in this relationship with you.

I'm glad you feel this way now. But your ecstasy will not last. It will not always be so clear to you.

Not true, I'm sure. I have found ecstasy, and I will never let it go! The line of people has come to an end, and Eric is saying a benediction. What has happened to me? Something has shifted inside. What is different? I can't tell, but surely nothing will ever be the same. A disquieting thought pops into mind: does this experience mean I can no longer hide my past? I had hoped that as a minister I could forget all those years of psychic experiences and being a New Age channel. Will I now have to face them after all? Some of the ecstasy is fading, replaced by tinges of fear.

5

PART I

CRYSTALS

1972–1983

Awakening

A s I look at my life prior to the mystical experience of 1994, it seems that everything led up to that moment.

It was early spring in 1972, a gray and overcast day that morning as I threw my tattered book bag into our dilapidated Volkswagen and took off for the University of Maryland campus. Richard Nixon was running for re-election, and Watergate had not yet reached the front pages of out daily paper, *The Washington Post*. I was a 25-year-old graduate student working on a doctorate degree in education, happily married to a doctoral student in the psychology department. We had chosen this univer-sity because it was the only one that offered both of us teaching assistantships for our doctoral programs. We had moved from the Midwest two years previously and set up housekeeping in a crowded, lower-income, brick apartment complex near campus.

I had no reason to think that this day would begin disturbing my comfortable agnosticism. Although raised Baptist—and later Presbyterian—I had given up religion in my senior year in high school after reading Ayn Rand and Nietzsche. I had decided I would rather search for truth than cling to the outmoded beliefs of my parents. I had no proof of a God and was too sophisticated to accept faith. My husband, Burt, agreed, although he felt certain there was no God and considered himself an atheist. As children of the sixties, we had a happy and comfortable lifestyle—getting together with friends to chat and hear music, listening to the Firesign Theater, attending periodic demonstrations against the Vietnam War in Washington, D.C., and supporting the presidential campaign of George McGovern in what little free time we had.

As I drove to campus that gray, spring day, I thought about the class I would be teaching. Each semester, I taught one or two sections of a required undergraduate course, "Social Foundations of Education." I loved teaching, and I especially loved that course since I had a chance to introduce America's future teachers to some innovative concepts. I encouraged my students to read *Summerhill* and John Holt and Paul Goodman. Local teachers in "free schools" came to class to talk about education. My sections of this course were popular and filled up quickly. This day we would be discussing some readings, and I thought about discussion questions I might use.

I approached the intersection that led into campus at my usual slow pace. I was a safe driver—so much so that, on this day, as I began pulling out of the intersection for a right turn, I saw a car coming too fast and slammed on my brakes to abort the turn. My body suddenly went rigid. The car behind me had slammed into my car's rear end. I had never been in an accident before. I wanted to drive off and pretend it hadn't happened.

But we exchanged license and insurance information. There was only minor damage to the car, and I seemed to be okay, a little shaken up maybe, but fine. I didn't know then that my life was about to change forever.

I arrived on campus a few minutes later, sore and somewhat traumatized. I taught class; being a workaholic, I would never have thought of canceling class just because of a minor auto accident. But I began feeling worse as the day progressed. Colleagues warned me about whiplash. I went to bed early but woke the next morning in misery, my back and neck burning with pain. I saw a doctor that day who said I had muscle spasms and gave me some tranquilizers, which I didn't take, not believing in medicine any more than I believed in God.

The following weeks were the most painful of my life. I had never had a backache in my twenty-five years; now, I had one constantly. The doctor said to be patient, that the pain would go away eventually. Everyone had advice: see a chiropractor, begin hatha yoga, meditate. I scoffed at such unscientific and "weird" cures. The weeks dragged on, and my pain continued. I consulted other doctors who also prescribed pills and patience. I began to feel abandoned by the medical profession. My father, a lawyer, called me from Illinois advising me to sue, at least to get medical expenses covered. On my behalf, he even began corresponding with the insurance company of the person who had hit my car.

My husband was caring, and friends were concerned. But I was miserable. I had never had such pain. In desperation, I even tried the prescribed pain pills, which brought only temporary relief since, as soon as they wore off, the pain was back.

I had scoffed at any healing outside of the medical profession, but I had become desperate. I didn't know if I'd get money for the accident, and we had little insurance coverage, so I wanted inexpensive relief. I finally decided to try the "weird" Eastern practice known as hatha yoga. I began watching a woman doing daily yoga exercises on the local educational channel. Soon, I was doing gentle backstretches. I was amazed that they not only helped more than the muscle relaxants prescribed by the doctor but that the effect lasted longer. I was incredulous that this was working, but soon yoga became part of my daily routine.

The yoga instructor taught breathing techniques and methods of relaxation. She ended her sessions with what she called "the sponge" position, where you just lie down in total relaxation and quiet. I had come to trust her wisdom, so followed her into that posture. At that point in my life, if she had called it "meditation," I would have refused to do it. But she didn't, so I did the routine every day.

After awhile, I became aware that those few minutes gave me a deep sense of tranquillity. My two or three minutes at the end of each session extended to fifteen or twenty minutes. Before I was aware that anything was changing, I began slipping into states where I suddenly *knew*. What I knew I couldn't put into words, but it had to do with realizing I was part of a whole—not a solitary, isolated, individual human being, but something beyond a body, something connected with cosmic wholeness. I felt it, and I knew.

I was profoundly embarrassed about what I was discovering and wouldn't discuss it with anyone. I was rational, logical, and scientific. I didn't believe in God or in Eastern nonsense like meditation. Yet, there I was doing yoga postures every day and slipping into these remarkable states in which I encountered something I had never known existed. I didn't want anyone to know. Even though my back kept getting better and I was becoming a more relaxed and serene person, I was a bit more withdrawn as I struggled with this embarrassing inner secret that was intruding upon my intellectualized graduate-school life.

I certainly did not want any further changes in my spiritual life. But those meditations of bliss were starting to wreak havoc for me. One morning I awoke early, noticing the curtain rods on the window right next to me and feeling the most profound peace I could ever remember. Then, I felt a thud and noticed that the window was quite a distance away and that the curtain rod was much higher than the bed. I had been floating by the window without my body. Impossible! I had been outside of my body. It was a wonderful experience. "So, we exist apart from our bodies," I thought, an idea that I dismissed as something to think about some day when I had more time.

But I could not postpone the thought for long. I seemed to be pursued by a force determined to break through my rationalistic shell. I found an intuitive self inside me to which I had never before been introduced. I began "knowing" things. For example, one day, as I was making airline reservations to visit my family in Illinois, I suddenly "knew" I shouldn't fly with American Airlines out of Washington, D.C., on that day. Scoffing at such nonsense, I booked the flight anyway and felt quite smug when I arrived without incident. On my arrival, my mother's first words to me were, "Thank God you're safe!

There was an American Airlines jet in D.C. that had an accident on the runway, and I was so afraid that was your plane!" What was this all about? How had I "known" that something would happen to an American Airlines flight in Washington, D.C., on that day? What was I supposed to do with that kind of "knowing? And who wants to "know," anyway? How could I get rid of that pesky intuition?

Soon, my intuitive thoughts changed from being merely annoying to being terrifying. As I lay in bed at night, I started hearing taps in my room. I awakened Burt to listen, but he heard nothing. The taps had a rhythm as though someone were trying to communicate, a sort of Morse Code, but I was frightened and refused to have anything to do with them.

Then, I began having emotions invade my mind that were related neither to my present adult life nor to my childhood. These feelings purportedly stemmed from scenes of other lifetimes. I "saw" myself in other places, other times; these scenes came to me as memories come, complete with feelings and associations attached.

I was beginning to fear for my sanity. However, I continued to function well at school. Burt and I approached the end of our course work and began writing our dissertations. Then, one night I awoke from a terrifying dream: I saw a fire on our table, burning in a perfect circle without consuming the table. It was so real that it took me a long time to get back to sleep. A few days later, I came in early from campus and recognized the smell of smoke as soon as I opened our apartment door. I ran in to find a pile of ashes on our dining room table in a near-perfect circle. There seemed to be no cause: nothing was on the table, and we had left no matches, candles, or appliances nearby. There was just

14

this circle of ashes in the middle of the table, as I had seen in my dream. I ran frantically back to campus to pull my husband away from the experiment he was working on. When we returned to the apartment, the pile was still there. He, too, was totally baffled since there seemed to be no human way such a fire could have started, burned, and then stopped. How could I have seen it in advance? I felt a panic building. Something was pursuing me. I had to give up meditation.

My yoga and meditation had led me into bliss, but that bliss had a price. It was opening up worlds I did not understand and did not want to know. I hated to give up those tranquil moments and allow the back pain to come back. But nothing was worth this fear. I stopped meditating.

I moved instead into a stage of complete resistance to the spiritual, attempting to close down centers that were rapidly opening. I tried to deny the bliss, the taps, the "past life" memories. I put a lot of psychic and intellectual energy into blocking. As a result, I became depressed, sick, and miserable with back pain. I knew that, eventually, I would have to face my internal blocks to the spiritual.

T W O

Purgation

On a cold day in January 1976, I headed through the New Haven rush-hour traffic for a 5PM appointment with a parapsychologist. I couldn't go on much longer without help. I had stopped meditating, but I couldn't stop the psychic and hypnagogic experiences that had invaded my life. My depression and anxiety were growing.

Fortunately, I had had much to occupy my mind in the months since ending my meditations. Burt and I had completed our doctoral course work and were well along on finishing our dissertations. Burt got a job offer in New Haven doing psychological research, so we moved from Washington, D.C., to Connecticut with plans to complete our dissertations there.

I had started attending the functions of a local spiritual growth center called the Prana Foundation. It seemed to be a very New Age, pro-psychic phenomena sort of place making efforts to bring legitimate research to people's spiritual and psychic experiences. The man who ran the center seemed practical and logical in his approach to the illogic of the psychic. After weeks of inner battles, I had finally made an appointment with him.

I drove through the congested New Haven streets in a state of mounting terror. I had never talked to anyone about my experiences, except my husband. I had finally confided in Burt and was relieved that, even though a psychology student and an atheist, he didn't think I was crazy. I wasn't so sure myself and hated to reveal this part of my being to anyone else. But I needed help. My efforts to stop the experiences weren't working; the psychic phenomena were getting worse, and I was feeling ever more miserable about apparently having no power to stop them. My hope was that the advisor at the Prana Foundation would tell me how to shut them off.

I was to be disappointed. I did find him to be a caring man, intensely involved with parapsychology and an active counseling practice where he used hypnotherapy. He was understanding and accepting of the reality of my bizarre experiences. He quickly perceived that my desire to stop them was a significant block to my growth and that my agnosticism was preventing me from accepting a world beyond the five senses. I wasn't, however, eager to listen. My doubts further surfaced in our second session when I told him I wasn't sure he could stop the experiences and might even cause them to increase.

I rebelled when my advisor suggested I try using prayer, particularly the Twenty-Third Psalm, and a white light. I told him I wasn't comfortable with the Bible and that I couldn't pray because I didn't believe in a personal God. His response forced me to reconsider my agnosticism.

He stated that there is energy contained in every cell of our bodies that we call God. When we say a prayer, what we're really trying to do is attain a state of harmony with cosmic consciousness, with all souls. Prayer is an exchange of the higher vibrations.

I liked and accepted this approach to God. It made sense to me that God was cosmic consciousness living in every cell of our bodies. I gave up my agnosticism at that point, but still had no intention of returning to Christianity. And I was certain that my new understanding of God would keep me outside of any established churches.

Slowly, I came to realize that I could not sustain my refusal to meditate. Those moments of tranquility had come to nourish my soul in a profound way, and I was depressed when I ignored them. My advisor at the Prana Foundation taught me ways to feel safe and told me I could call him anytime, day or night, if I became frightened.

I returned to meditation and even tried hypnotherapy to explore some of my psychic experiences. As I gained greater confidence, my advisor talked to me about psychic channeling and about the important service channelers could perform in being of help to others. He emphasized the importance of being in a state of love and of giving oneself over to the service of God. After a period of weeks, I found myself able to go into a trance state and write words of spiritual assurance and guidance, a process that is called "automatic writing." With my advisor's help, I learned that I didn't need to write the words, since they were coming into my head. So, in a trance state, I began to speak the words. I was developing into a channel.

My conflicts about what I was doing were intense. I was obsessed with finding evidence that what I was experiencing was a genuine psychic phenomenon and not my imagination. I wanted proof that the information was coming from outside myself, and therefore was "authentic." Yet I worried that something from outside could cause possession, and I was frightened.

My advisor sought guidance from a well-known trance medium visiting the New Haven area. I received a reading that still moves me twenty years later, a reading that spoke of past lives and present guilt. The reading was tape-recorded and transcribed, so I can provide the highlights of this experience.

I was told that a number of influences were working in my psyche, some from "soul memory" and some from my present experience with universal forces and attitudes that I held regarding my own self-worth. The reading indicated that I felt a need to be punished because of past transgressions, that I felt I could not accomplish any good until I had suffered for my "control of others in the past," especially through the use of occult or psychic forces.

The reading was adamant that I had to work on establishing a sense of self-worth, a sense of being acceptable as I was in my present personality. I also had to train and orient my mind to understand that the higher influences of psychic forces need not come only from without the self but can come as well from within.

Thus, the reading outlined for me what I needed to do before I could fully develop as a channel: I needed to work on my self-esteem issues, to stop trying to contact something outside myself, and to learn to look within for guidance. The reading also identified the elements of an eating disorder and recommended a number of changes in my diet. Then I could return to channeling, a channeling that looked to the highest sources within myself.

With twenty years of hindsight, I see this reading as the heart of what I needed to learn at the beginning of my purification period. I did learn some of it, enough to continue into the next stage of illumination. But the bulk of work I had to do was left for the "dark night." And some of it continues to be done. But, at that point, the trance source was right. If I tried to develop as a psychic channeler without a solid sense of self, I would be destroyed by forces I would be inviting into myself.

I quit trance work for awhile, focusing on meditation and prayer. It was clear that I had a lot of work to do on myself as part of my spiritual journey.

T H R E E

Illumination

After the trance reading that took place in early 1978, I quit automatic writing for awhile, focusing on meditation and prayer. I worked on my self-esteem, but had yet to reclaim memories of trauma from childhood or to recognize the impact that my eating disorder had on me. I did see a nutritionist and stayed on a better diet for awhile, supplemented by vitamins and minerals that also helped.

I addressed my issues on a superficial level. Everything seemed to look up for me. I got a new job as a drug counselor. I finished my doctorate in Social Foundations of Education and became "Dr. Wake."

After an intensive ten months of hypnotherapy and supportive counseling with my advisor at the Prana Foundation, I was ready to face the world again. I felt composed and strong, with my fears gone. My reading had taught me the importance of going within my self, and I finally got the message.

21

As my self-confidence increased and my health improved, I felt ready to return to channeling. My advisor had a new plan in mind: he advertised in the foundation's newsletter for people to have readings through the foundation. He had me and another psychic-in-training give the readings, while he assessed them for accuracy.

I was quite uneasy about doing readings for other people, but my advisor was encouraging and offered to serve as an evaluator. The process began slowly; but as I became relaxed, more and more information flowed out. I felt I was contacting my higher self rather than a spirit entity. In that state, I found I could access facts about people that I could not have known consciously.

Trance work became one of my greatest joys. I found I could easily slip into a trance state, where I felt mild bliss. My husband would ask questions, sometimes general ones about life, sometimes specific ones about the people who came for readings. He would write my words down as I spoke, and I would type them later. My reputation as a psychic grew in the New Haven area. I had frequent requests for readings and occasionally for help with something like a haunted house.

I also meditated twice each day. Meditation had again become an experience of great peace and sometimes one of deep joy. At times, meditation held surprises, such as when I seemed to receive a visit from my grandmother, who had been dead for several years. She asked for help in adjusting to the "other side" and wanted to thank my mother for her prayers. My sense of her presence was extremely vivid and real to me; but I hesitated to give the message to my mother, whom I knew did not believe in praying for the dead. I was astounded to find that mom was pleased with the message and had, indeed, been praying for grandma for some time.

One night I had a dream in which I was writing a book. So vivid was the dream that the next day I began putting the journal of my work with the Prana Foundation into readable form; soon the journal began circulating among the foundation's members and my friends. I received much positive feedback on it, as many people found it useful in their own spiritual journeys, and was encouraged to try to have it published. With mixed feelings, I mailed it to a few publishers and got, as I expected, rejections, although some were warm and encouraging. I gave up on publication, only to find that the father of a friend had read it. The man was a distributor for Belmont-Tower Books. He mailed the manuscript to the publisher, and the next thing I knew I had a phone call from an editor, wanting to sign a contract for a book.

Life again changed quickly. I had no idea how the publishing process unfolded and was busy making final revisions and talking with the editor. I couldn't imagine what it would be like to have my story in print, but I asked to have it published under a pseudonym, because of my hesitation in relating these extraordinary occurrences.

In the meantime, my advisor was leaving the presidency of the Prana Foundation to go full-time into private practice. I was recommended to the board of directors as his replacement, and I was voted in on the spot. Suddenly, I was running a foundation. I quit my job, although I actually made very little money at Prana. The president's job was a sort of all-purpose position: I did counseling, as well as hypnotic regressions, readings, and spiritual consultations. I ran groups, organized workshops, coordinated potluck dinners, and kept the toilet paper in the bathroom and the floors swept. I was increasingly feeling like a minister of a New Age congregation. I loved the role and felt sad that I could never be ordained in a church, given my beliefs.

When my first book, *Beyond the Body,* was published in 1979, life became a whirlwind. The publishers set up a number of interviews on the East Coast—primarily on radio talk shows, with one or two on television. I received numerous invitations to give lectures and workshops. Several hundred letters came in about the book, many from people wanting readings or help with their spiritual lives.

Life should have been perfect, but I was troubled by the new role I found myself in. I had quickly become a leader in my local New Age community, but I had no training, credentials, or background for my job. My primary qualification seemed to be my channeling, but I was constantly aware of the fallibility of it. I was uncomfortable by how often people coming for readings would push for very specific pieces of information. When would they meet their ideal mate? Should they put their house on the market? When would they die? Where had they lost a piece of jewelry? My trance self often sidetracked these questions and instead gave long lectures on faith and spiritual growth. Its style was to identify the areas of spiritual conflict in a person, then to focus on how those issues were operating in the present, and finally to offer general directions for future growth.

I increasingly felt overburdened by the responsibilities in my new role as foundation president, psychic channeler, counselor, public speaker, and author. I was actually relieved when, in 1980, Burt and I considered moving. I was making little money at my work, and Burt had just finished being trained as a clinical psychologist. He could not find a job in the New Haven area, so we decided to look in New Hampshire and Vermont. We dreamed of a place in the country where we could become self-sufficient and prepare for the many earth changes being predicted.

We were thrilled when Burt got a job in New Hampshire in the spring of 1980. It was hard to leave our many friends and colleagues in Connecticut, but I was relieved to give up my role there. I thought I'd like to live in the country and just write and garden. We moved to New Hampshire, and soon found a dream place in the country—a small, rustic, saltbox house with wood-beam ceilings and a passive solar design. Making the mortgage payments was difficult on Burt's salary, so I decided to start offering workshops in Concord.

I discovered that my book had been selling there, and some people had heard of me. My meditation classes filled up quickly, and soon there was a large group wanting to meet on a regular basis. We started having large weekly gatherings where I would sometimes lead meditations and sometimes bring in speakers. Our numbers grew regularly, with about forty people coming each week. Many of them asked for readings with me, and I was kept busy channeling. Some who received readings asked for counseling, and I found myself drifting into the role of therapist. Although I felt competent teaching meditation and encouraging spiritual growth, my clients increasingly had far more complex problems, such as depression. I was out of my depth. Again, I was back in the business of leading groups, giving readings, counseling, and feeling like a minister, yet having no church, no faith tradition, no training. Since ordination was not possible for me in any church I could imagine, I thought about going back to school—perhaps for a doctorate in psychology. In 1981, my second book was published, *Beyond the Mind*, which explored further the areas of the psychic for counseling and psychology. Again, I published under a pseudonym. I shudder now as I read what I was doing and writing before I had any training in counseling or ministry. But the book added to my reputation in the New Age community.

I was coming unglued, however. I couldn't keep up that role any longer without training. Yet, I wasn't sure I could manage returning to school since my health was deteriorating. I spent many days each month home in bed with one virus after another. Believing in holistic medicine, I went to a holistic physician in Boston who diagnosed candida (intestinal yeast infections) as well as numerous food allergies. I was once again put on many vitamins and a strict diet. I had much more energy on a diet free of my food allergens and my health began to improve.

Believing in a body/mind connection, I decided to find a counselor. I began work with a pastoral counselor, thinking such a person would understand my psychic experiences and spiritual life. He helped me identify my sense of call to ministry. Needing a church to be accepted for ministry, I went to our local Unitarian-Universalist (UU) church and signed up for membership. Since the UUs are open to all spiritual paths, I figured they would accept mine.

In many ways, I liked being a Unitarian-Universalist and was relieved that I wasn't asked questions about what I believed. I started Boston University School of Theology in January 1983, feeling proud of my minority non-Christian status. I was a Unitarian who was not a Christian, and I was rather offended by all of the Christian symbols—such as crosses—all over the seminary. On the other hand, I had trouble integrating my mysticism with the UUs I met. I ran into people who were rationalists and humanists who viewed mysticism as suspiciously as I viewed Christianity.[1]

Work with my pastoral counselor was helping me look at some of those issues and, under his influence, I was persuaded to visit some Christian churches. I decided to visit an Episcopal Church. It was my first experience of communion where everyone would go to the altar, kneel, receive wafers, then be offered a common wine chalice. In my Baptist and Presbyterian traditions—which I hadn't observed in years—wafers and little glasses of grape juice were passed among the worshipers pew by pew. In those traditions, the communion was generally seen as a symbol of our relationship with Christ. In the Episcopal tradition, however, many communicants had a belief in a real spiritual presence in the bread and wine after the priest consecrated them.

I thought this belief sounded utterly bizarre, but I wanted to experience this unusual tradition. After kneeling and receiving the wafer and chalice, I began making my way back to my pew. A sudden rush of energy suffused my being with feelings of warmth and love. It was similar to the trance energy I was accustomed to, but it was far more powerful and imbued with what seemed to be pure Love. I sat at my pew and felt the energy vibrating through me. I thought, "Is this what Christians experience at communion? I never knew!" I was incredulous that, after all of my years of meditation

---

1. This is nor necessarily typical of UUs. I've since met many UU mystics.

and trance work, a far deeper energy was so easily and readily available.

I began skipping Unitarian services on Sunday mornings to slip into the Episcopal Church for a new rush of love, peace, energy, and vitality. Eucharist could clearly become addictive. Having discovered it, I didn't think I could ever live without it. Despite my discovery, I continued in my solid non-Christian stance at theology school.

Several months into the spring term of 1983, Holy Week came. I didn't pay much attention to the week prior to Easter since I wasn't a Christian. But that year, I realized that, during Holy Week, I could receive the Eucharist by attending an Episcopal service each day. I began attending a daily service, and my life changed forever.

The energy during this week seemed to penetrate deeper than before and seemed more personal. I felt myself truly in the presence of a loving being and knew that I was not alone. I felt my heart melting in some mysterious way as the week progressed.

On Maundy Thursday, I was at the theology school that day and night. I kept a room near the school and stayed over a couple nights a week, Thursday being one of my regular nights to stay there. I went to a local Episcopal Church for an early evening service and received the Eucharist and then, filled with love and peace, went back to my room. Suddenly, everything changed. I was not alone in my room; a figure stood there. I saw him not with my physical eyes, but rather my spiritual ones; yet, in my mind, I saw him clearly and felt his energy radiating throughout the room. I knew it was Christ. His energy was so overwhelmingly powerful and loving that I was transfixed. With all of my psychic encounters, I had never before come in contact with a being that seemed so pure and divine. I could do only one thing. Instinctively, I knelt at his feet and bowed my head.

He put his hand on my head, and spoke to me. Again I heard with inner ears, but with total clarity:

I am calling you into my service. I want you to be a minister in my name.

There was only one response possible.

Yes, of course. Whatever you want me to do. Just tell me, and I'll do it.

I felt energy radiating from his hands into my bowed head.

I am ordaining you now for my service, but I also want you to seek ordination in a church.

Which church, I wondered. There was no answer, just energy coming from his hands. However, I interpreted the silence to mean the Episcopal Church, since it was in the context of the Eucharist there that I had first felt Christ's presence.

After a few moments, the image faded, but the energy remained. I knew that something profound had just happened to me, and that I was changed forever. What was different now? I had just committed myself to Jesus Christ, and I had agreed to become a Christian minister. Did that also mean I was now a Christian? Is that what it meant to be a Christian? Whatever the answer, I knew I had no option but to seek ordination as a Christian. I would become Episcopalian, and spend the rest of my life as a priest consecrating the elements for Eucharist.

It was hard to go back to my seminary friends and

admit that one of the staunchest non-Christians of the school had just converted. I felt I couldn't begin to put into words why or how, except to say that there was something about Holy Week and the Eucharist that had won me over. My friends were very happy for me and welcomed me into their faith. My therapist was also extremely pleased for me, but urged me to be cautious about switching denominations from Unitarian to Episcopalian after just beginning seminary studies. I thought that advice was silly, since I was certain that the power of my personal experience was a call to Episcopal priesthood and a promise that the ordination process would go smoothly.

I resigned from the Unitarian-Universalists and sought to join the New Hampshire Episcopal Church that I had been attending. I spoke with an Episcopal priest about a call to ordination, signed up for confirmation classes, and met with the bishop of our diocese. It was clear that the step from Unitarianism to Episcopalianism was going to be a big one. I had no idea how to integrate my work as a psychic channel with my desire to be an Episcopal priest. Still, all my experiences made sense to me, since I felt they all had to do with channeling God's energy. I didn't know, however, just how an established church would view that. But I trusted that, if Christ were calling me, he would smooth the way.

The bishop asked me to transfer to the Episcopal Divinity School, so I applied there for the fall term of 1983. I would have to study for three full years there, but that seemed fine—just being on a campus that had a daily Eucharist sounded like heaven! I had arranged to be confirmed at my parish's scheduled service with the bishop in May of 1983.

My confirmation day stands out as one of the high-

lights of my mystical career. I had few expectations of the
service, other than that each of us would kneel in front of
the bishop, he would put his hands on each head and say
some words, and then there was a Eucharist. I was again
stunned to discover the power in a traditional ritual,
however. As I knelt and the bishop put his hands on my
head, I could actually feel energy coming from his hands
into my being, energy that had reality and changed my
inner self in some mysterious way I could not identify.

After my final semester at the Boston University
School of Theology, with more time during the summer
months, I did more psychic readings for people, feeling
more than ever that readings were something sacred, just
as the Eucharist was. One woman I channeled for that
summer had recently read one of my books and was extremely pleased with my trance words. As it happened,
she was an Episcopalian and excited to hear that I had
joined the Episcopal Church and was seeking ordination. She felt that what I represented was what the
church needed. So, she sent a copy of my book to the
bishop.

Somehow, I wasn't so sure that action spelled good
news for me in my effort to be ordained. Some months
later, I learned that my feeling was accurate.

In the fall of 1983, as I began my studies at Episcopal Divinity School in Boston, life seemed great. I had a
warm and wonderful husband who was devoted to my
seminary studies. I was in an excellent seminary, able to
receive the Eucharist daily. My private practice in counseling and readings was flourishing in New Hampshire.
Perhaps it was fortunate that I hadn't a hint of the next
stage on the spiritual journey, referred to by many as a
dark night of the soul.

REFLECTIONS ON THE PAST
Crystals

At the time of my initial psychic experiences in the 1970s, I had no idea what was happening, and I feared that perhaps I was going crazy. I had no basis on which to make sense out of this dimension of life. I feared reading about the spiritual experiences of others, certain that my own would seem incredibly insignificant by comparison. Then, at some point after many years of spiritual reflection, I came to realize that what was happening to me wasn't about my personal experiences. What matters is the process by which humanity encounters divinity. Every individual story is unique, but the larger story of how God brings us into the divine relationship is universal and has been told again and again. As I came to watch the themes of this story emerging in my own life, I found myself resonating with the spiritual unfolding in the lives of others.

My early spiritual journey of meditations and channeling was one in which I moved from being an agnostic to having a mystical knowing of God's existence. I had found ecstasy in meditation, but also encountered fear. I reached a point where only self-examination would move me further along the spiritual path. There are a variety of perspectives to use in interpreting this phase of my journey. In the following pages and at the end of each phase of my development, I offer my current evaluation from the advantage of hindsight. As with all things, this perspective is constantly evolving.

NEW-AGE PERSPECTIVES

As I look now at the trance reading and the help I received from my advisor at the Prana Foundation, I can't help but think how time- and culture-bound it all was. Had I lived in a different society or time, I would have received very different help. In some time periods, my experiences would have been classified as "witchcraft." Had I gone to a spiritual director—particularly one with a mystical orientation—I might have been oriented towards some traditional Christian practices and values.

But in the United States of the 1970s, we baby boomers were discovering spirituality and were jumping full-speed ahead into the New Age. Many of us walked out of our childhood religions into the spiritual remnants of the political counterculture of the 1960s. We still believed that our generation could do anything better than anyone before us, and we were determined to discover our own spirituality for our own time. What we developed had elements of traditional mysticism but in a new blend that we saw as unique to us. For many of us, our priests and gurus were the psychic channelers. The call to become a channel was probably, to us, comparable to the traditional calls to ministry or priesthood or some form of religious life. It was our religion. For me at that time, it was the only one I would have allowed to help me through my crisis.

I realize now that, in rejecting traditional religion to guide our spiritual journeys, many of us also cut off an understanding of mystical knowing.

I write these words as one who provided some leadership in the 1970s and 1980s, without an inkling that psychic channeling was other than the ultimate in spiritual development. I knew nothing of mystical traditions that taught adherents how to avoid getting stuck in "psychic phenomena" and move into the deeper spirituality beyond.

At that point, my New-Age supporters saw my journey as one in which I was opening to channeling. This opening process was generally affirmed in the New-Age community and seen as positive spiritual development and a vital way to be of service to others. To be a channel in the 1970s was seen as being in touch with divine wisdom, but I feared that many took my trance statements to be more valid than they actually were. After my books were released, I felt I was seen as having access to special forms of information. I suspected that clients of mine ignored their own inner sources of information in favor of mine. In her work *Anatomy of the Spirit: The Seven Stages of Power and Healing*, medical intuitive Caroline Myss talks about a sudden realization in a workshop that people were becoming too dependent on her intuition and ignoring their own.[1] At that point, she began teaching others how to access their own resources.

With similar feelings of wanting to develop a ministry that helped people connect with their own spirituality, I was off to seminary, all the while still adhering to my psychic counseling. Yet, I was still ignorant of exactly what I hoped to accomplish in my ministry, as evidenced by my embracing Unitarian-Universalism and then abandoning it for the more orthodox Episcopalianism.

CHRISTIAN MYSTICISM

Over the years, I have been drawn to read about the experiences of other mystics, to see if my personal journey in any way corresponds to the experience of others. Obviously, there will be individual differences and even different choices, but I hoped to find an understanding of the Way by examining the paths of others.

In reviewing the early years of my journey—the disquietude of spirit and fear of insanity as well as the exultation and profound discoveries—I found analogies in the symbolism described by TERESA OF AVILA. In her extraordinary work, Teresa of Avila, one of the most-revered Christian mystics, speaks of the spiritual journey

---

1. Carolyn Myss, *Anatomy of the Spirit: The Seven Stages of Power and Healing* (New York: Three Rivers Press, 1996).

within as moving through an interior castle.[2] The court-yard of the castle is filled with venomous creatures. The castle, she says, is the soul with many rooms, and not everyone enters its portals to make the journey. For those who do, the gateway to the first mansion is gener-ally prayer and meditation. In this first room, or man-sion, the souls are still in love with sin, still connected with the creatures outside. They stay here a long time to learn discipline and humility. Teresa sees the soul as a garden where God has pulled up the weeds and planted flowers in their place. Our task from God is to water the garden by prayer. It is natural for us to resist prayer, but we must be determined to continue.

Teresa talks of the soul entering the second man-sion, to hear the beauty of God's voice calling, but to also encounter its own evil. Reptiles are there, and God may allow them to bite so that the soul can learn and be-come stronger. There will be urges to turn back, but it is important to continue, seeking help if necessary. This is the mansion of practicing prayer and other spiritual dis-ciplines. Our prayer life might have periods of aridity, but it is important to persevere. Then, in the third man-sion, the soul attempts to avoid venial sins and engage in prayer of recollection, where it examines its conscience and confesses sins.

Part of this intense spiritual period involved feel-ings of tremendous ecstasy in my spiritual life. Teresa un-derstood about a spiritual stage that is filled with ecstasies

2. Teresa of Avila, *The Interior Castle*, trans. Kieran Kavanaugh and Otillio Rodriguez (New York: Paulist Press, 1979). Another edition of this work that I recommend is *The Interior Castle by St. Teresa of Avila*, translated and edited by E. Allison Peers (New York: Image Books, 1961).

and delights. She calls it the fourth dwelling place and says that supernatural experiences begin in this place. At this point, less is happening by personal effort, and more by God's intervention; this could correspond with my ecstatic trance experiences. Teresa states that the seeker should develop an established prayer life here, which she calls the Prayer of Quiet, which comes from the person's deepest core and brings peace, quiet, and joy. It is as though Christ enters the soul to speak as a friend. Contemplation begins and guides the self into the fifth dwelling place, filled with great riches, treasures, and delights. In this mansion, the Spiritual Betrothal takes place and the Prayer of Union begins. In this prayer, the mystic's faculties become dim as he or she enters a trance-like state of meditation. God enters deep into the soul and allows a union experience that leaves the person convinced that there has been an encounter with God. Like a betrothal, the prayer moves the soul closer to union with the Divine. I have often thought that this could be what I found in the Eucharist: a Spiritual Betrothal with the Lord.

EVELYN UNDERHILL, a scholar who studied the mystical journeys of visionaries throughout history, says that spiritual seekers often begin with an awakening of the self, which involves a shifting of consciousness to a higher level.[3]

According to Underhill, many mystics then encounter a period, which she calls "purification of the self." During this period, which Underhill explains can last for a lifetime, the mystic must face personal inadequacy for

---

3. Evelyn Underhill, *Mysticism: The Preeminent Study in the Nature and Development of Spiritual Consciousness* (New York: Doubleday, 1990), 196.

making the journey but yet find the inner thirst for God that makes it impossible to stop the journey. This is "purgation," an early stage in a long process of purification, in which one may move back and forth from periods of bliss to feeling pain.[4] Both Teresa's castle rooms and Underhill's stages of spiritual growth describe for me the awakening of my spiritual self and the need to begin looking at the issues within that could block union with the Divine. I was practicing spiritual disciplines, but not comprehending love.

Underhill also wrote about a stage that corresponds to Teresa's Spiritual Betrothal, calling it the "Illumination of Self." She describes this stage as a swing back into sunlight after a tough period of purgation. The mystic is falling in love in this stage. There is still an "I" existing, but it is an "I" in love with the Divine. It is a time in which the seeker feels a great deal of joy and in which his or her intuition is enhanced as psychic experiences abound—including visions, voices, dialogues with beings, and automatic writing:

> In illumination we come to that state of consciousness which is popularly supposed to be peculiar to the mystic: a form of mental life, a kind of perception, radically different from that of "normal" men. . . . The self emerges from long and varied acts of purification to find that it is able to apprehend another order of reality. It has achieved consciousness of a world that was always there, and wherein its substantial being—that Ground which is of God—has always stood. Such a consciousness is "Transcendental Feeling" *in excelsus:* a deep, intuitional knowledge of the "secret plan."[5]

---

4. Underhill, 198–204.
5. Underhill, 232–233.

As you will see, the mystic whom I admire most is EMANUEL SWEDENBORG. In many ways, Swedenborg and I are different. He was an upperclass male living from 1688 to 1772, a brilliant scientist. Swedenborg was in his fifties when God began calling him into close relationship. That process transformed his life from one of world-renowned scientist to great psychic, mystic, and theologian, who has been both much revered and greatly criticized. The specifics of my life are very different, and my spiritual experiences seem as nothing compared to his. But when I read his story of a human being encountering the Divine, I find universal themes that help me understand my own spiritual process.

In 1743, Swedenborg started keeping a journal as he traveled. At first, he recorded the places he visited and people he met, as many tourists do. Then, suddenly, he began writing down his dreams. The early ones seemed to be about travel. Wilson Van Dusen, psychologist, author, and commentator on Swedenborg's *Journal of Dreams*, surmises that these dreams were "speaking of *travel* as journeying in this inner realm."[6] Swedenborg began commenting about having ecstatic experiences and wakeful trances. Van Dusen explains that, as a young man, Swedenborg practiced a form of intense concentration and meditation that was almost trance-like. His breathing slowed down, so he came to understand *pranayana*, or a kind of breath control that has been practiced by yogis of the East for many centuries. Van Dusen speculates that Swedenborg would not have had access to the Hindu literature, so must have discovered

6. *Swedenborg's Journal of Dreams*, 1743–1744, translated by J. J. G. Wilkinson, with commentary by Wilson Van Dusen (New York: Swedenborg Foundation, 1986), 17.

pranayana on his own, remarking, *"To my mind this is the single most important, unusual thing that Swedenborg did; it led to an immense flowering of inner experience."*[7]

Is it possible that Swedenborg, too, began his spiritual quest by meditating? The yoga and breathing I was being taught were from ancient traditions. Had Swedenborg also tapped into these traditions, and begun his spiritual awakening in a similar way?

There was certainly some similarity in how the awakening unfolded. My meditations were leading me into ecstasies and into strange experiences that happened at night before I fell asleep, when I awoke during the night, or in the morning. Swedenborg seemed to have a great deal of this type of phenomena. He noted in his journal entry number 14 that his trances were often before and after sleep.

Van Dusen believes that Swedenborg's trances before and after sleep are what is now called the hypnagogic state,[8] in which the dreamer lingers between sleep and awakening. In this state, we can see very clear imagery and even hear voices. Awakening completely, however, causes it to vanish. But it is a time of remarkably lucid thinking.

This period of channeling was a difficult period for me, but I receive some comfort from knowing that Swedenborg faced similar battles in his spiritual journey. I had stopped meditation and become depressed. Swedenborg had, in some way, tried to defy the spirit and found that life lost its meaning, as he writes in his journal entry number 13:

7. Ibid., 18. The italics are Van Dusen's.
8. Ibid., 21.

And how I set myself against the spirit.

And how I then favored it, but found afterwards that it was madness, devoid of all life and connection.

And that thus a quantity of what I have written must be of the same kind; because I had not at all resisted the power of the spirit to that degree; inasmuch as the faults are all my own, but the truths are not mine.

Indeed I sometimes fell into impatience and into thoughts [doubts], and would fain have given way to insolent demand whenever the matter did not go so easily as I wished, as I did nothing for my own sake: but I was a long way from finding out my own unworthiness, or being grateful for mercies.

Thus, Swedenborg, too, tried to run away from encounters with the Divine, only to find God in pursuit of the relationship. As Van Dusen paraphrases journal entry number 23 : "I found myself in a royal place, but I went out because I was not worthy. To my surprise the royal lady came to me anyway. . . ."[9] In other dreams, Swedenborg feels trapped, as in entry number 19, where he is in a garden and desperately tries to figure a way to escape.

Swedenborg also found himself confronting evil when he tried to resist the Lord, as he shows in entry number 15:

> How I set myself against the power of the Holy Spirit, what happened thereupon; how I saw hideous spectres, without life horribly shrouded and moving in their shrouds; together with a beast that attacked me. . . .

---

9. Ibid., 27.

And, finally, Swedenborg, too, realized that he needed help, as he records in entry number 20:

> Descended a great staircase . . . . Signifies the danger I am in of falling into hell, if I do not get help.

Van Dusen points out how quickly Swedenborg is able to recognize that he needs help and becomes open to it. The psychologist interprets journal entry number 23 in which Swedenborg is ashamed of his being "shabbily dressed and having no wig" when he is standing in a magnificent room as the dreamer's beginning to discover the humility of his own unworthiness, in Van Dusen's paraphrase, "I am in a high and spiritual place. I feel unworthy."[10] Thus, for Swedenborg, this was not an easy period.

Finally, Swedenborg was adamant that spiritual seekers should not seek out conversations with departed spirits, believing that his own angelic and demonic conversations were allowed by the Lord only so that humanity could know the truth of the spiritual world. Had I known of Swedenborg at the time of my channeling, his words would have validated my fear that I could be encountering evil and supported my decision to stop channeling while I addressed my personal and spiritual issues.

My own journey was one in which I experienced great ecstasy, but then found that my spirituality took a dramatic turn towards Christian mysticism. I think that Swedenborg, too, had a similar period in his spiritual journey, albeit one that was, of course, of far greater

---

10. Ibid., 28.

depth than mine. In his journal, he records the following
about entry number 44:

> Afterwards I wakened and slept again many times,
> and all was in answer to my thoughts, yet in such
> wise that there was a life and such a glory in all
> that I can give no account of it in the least; for it
> was all heavenly; clear for me at the time; but af-
> terwards I can explain nothing of it. In a word, I
> was in heaven and heard speech that no human
> tongue with the life in it can utter; nor the glory
> and innermost delight in the train of the speech.
>
> Except this I was in a waking state, as in a
> heavenly ecstasy, which also is indescribable.

Then, in entry number 48, he writes:

> Had also in my mind and my body a kind of
> consciousness of an indescribable bliss, so that if it
> had been in a higher degree, the body would have
> been as it were dissolved in mere bliss. . . .

Wilson Van Dusen thinks that, during this period,
Swedenborg came to know trance states, in which he experienced prayers being put into his mouth. Van Dusen,
who is himself a mystic, says of trance states, "You find
you are saying something, but a little reflection shows
the words formed of themselves. It was given to you.
This has happened so often to me that I finally con-
cluded all speech is of this nature. This is what Swedenborg would later call influx from heaven."[11]
    One of the reasons that I have found Swedenborg
to be such a helpful mentor for my own journey is that
his mysticism took a decidedly Christian direction, as

---

11. Ibid., 47.

did mine. Those familiar with his life know well of the dramatic events that transformed him during Easter week of 1744. He had been to church on April 6, attending Easter services and receiving communion. The next day, traveling to Delft, he experienced great bliss. That night, "he suddenly was seized with such trembling that he fell from his bed onto the floor. There, feeling wide awake, he experienced a Christ-vision. He found himself cradled in Jesus' arms and felt that he had been divinely commissioned to a special work."[12] At this point, Swedenborg's life was transformed. This crucial step in his journey changed him from scientist to theologian. I feel that he would understand the rational, academic "me" working on a doctorate degree, the woman who discovered God and later had an intense encounter with Christ. And, during all of that, I moved away from my original academic goals to train in ministry.

Two areas of spiritual growth that Swedenborg deals with are *repentance* and *regeneration*, both of which have relevance to my experience. I think the early stages described by Teresa and other mystics and explained by Underhill are similar to the first stage of spiritual growth that Swedenborg identified, that of repentance. In his final volume on theology, published just one year before his death, he wrote:

> The Lord is charity and faith in man, and man is charity and faith in the Lord. But it is asked, How can man enter into this union? The reply is that he cannot, unless to some extent he removed his

---

12. George F. Dole and Robert H. Kirven, *A Scientist Explores Spirit*, second edition (West Chester, Penna.: Chrysalis Books, 1997), 39.

evils by repentance. It is said that man must remove them, because this is not done by the Lord
directly, apart from man's co-operation. . . .

True Christian Religion 522[13]

In another passage (*True Christian Religion* 561), he states
that actual repentance involves examining oneself, rec-
ognizing one's sins, and beginning a new life by confessing the sins before God. I had worked with an advisor and
was moving into a period of self-examination, through
the modern means of self-discovery known as therapy.

The New-Age theorists would say that I was opening my psychic centers. Teresa would say that I had been
in the first five rooms of the castle, where I had to examine myself. Swedenborg, I think, would say both of
these had happened, but that only by walking through
repentance would I be able to begin the spiritual journey
he calls regeneration.

More precisely, according to Swedenborg's schema
of spiritual growth, I had moved into a stage he refers to
as "reformation" at that point in my life. As he explains
in *True Christian Religion* 571, reformation is the stage
during which one "looks from his natural to the spiritual
state and longs for that state. In the second stage [re-
generation], he becomes spiritual-natural." Swedenborg
compares regeneration to a silkworm, drawing out fila-
ments of silk; later, it will fly. He also uses the analogy of
a spring day: reformation is the dawn of the day or the
crowing of the cock, while regeneration is the day ad-
vancing to its fullness.

---

13. As is customary in Swedenborgian studies, the numbers following titles refer to paragraph or section numbers, which are uniform in
all editions, rather than to page numbers.

In *True Christian Religion* 572, Swedenborg also says of reformation that it is being born again, of water and spirit. This scriptural reference signifies that one is born by "means of truths of faith and a life in accordance with them." To Swedenborg, being born again, as described in the Scriptures, refers to the process of regeneration. I had begun to walk the path of new birth.

I did not know at the time, however, that this ecstasy-filled stage would not last forever. I thought I had found eternal bliss, but had not yet read Swedenborg or Teresa or even Evelyn Underhill to know of the stages yet ahead.

But I had moved out of my New Age "crystal" stage and was into the realm of Christian mysticism. As I attempted to integrate the New Age with Christian mysticism, I would have much to learn about crosses.

QUESTIONS FOR
JOURNALING AND DISCUSSION

1. Have you had any periods of spiritual awakening? If so, how did you become aware of the presence of spirit in your life. If not, what could you do that would help you take the initial steps out of Teresa's courtyard into the first mansion?

2. Have you embarked on a spiritual process of examining your conscience, confessing your errors, and making a new start? If so, how did that process affect your spiritual growth? If not, read about Teresa's third mansion or Swedenborg's explanation of repentance and use their guidance to undertake such a step.

3. Have you had any periods in your spiritual journey that were filled with joy and delight? If so, examine them and the impact they had on your relationship with the Divine.

4. Have you experienced a peaceful "Prayer of Quiet?" What was it like for you? If you have not had such an experience, read about Teresa's fourth mansion or use guides on meditation and prayer to help you.

5. Have you encountered a kind of rebirth? What has this meant for you? What further changes do you see in your spiritual quest?

PART 2

CROSSES

1983–1994

Wilderness Wandering

I call this period a wilderness wandering, although the traditional Christian term is a "dark night of the soul." The term "wilderness wandering" reminds me of the Israelites who wandered in the desert, having their faith tested, as they sought the Promised Land. I've used wilderness wandering to refer to my own experience, but still quote Underhill and the mystics in their own words. As Underhill explained,

> The most intense period of that great swing-back into darkness which usually divides the "first mystic life," or Illuminative Way, from the "second mystic life," or Unitive Way, is generally a period of utter blankness and stagnation, so far as mystical activity is concerned. The "Dark Night of the Soul," once fully established, is seldom lit by visions or made

homey by voices. It is of the essence of its miseries that the once-possessed power of orison or contemplation now seems wholly lost. The self is tossed back from its hard-won point of vantage. Impotence, blankness, solitude are the epithets by which those immersed in this dark fire of purification describe their pains.[1]

This period of my life is still recent, with much of it raw and undigested. Many of my experiences involve the lives of other people who deserve to have their privacy respected, so I will be brief here. But my brevity in writing is not a reflection of the pain of this period—more intense than I had yet encountered—or its length, which was over ten years.

I date this stage's beginning in January of 1983 as I was starting my second semester at Episcopal Divinity School in Cambridge. I remember how much I valued our Curriculum Conference there, which was a weekly gathering of a small group of first-year students with a faculty advisor and a senior student as mentor. Our mentor was a man named Jim, a wonderfully mystical man who helped me feel welcome in the Episcopal Church with my psychic leanings. One of the other students in the conference was Anne, an advocate of holistic health, and we had a great time giving our conference controversial questions about theology.

It was during that January that Jim referred to an article he had just read about issues of childhood trauma. I found myself starting to sob as I suddenly remembered events of my childhood that had remained deeply buried in my psyche. When I saw my pastoral counselor that

---

1. Evelyn Underhill, *Mysticism*, 381.

week, I told him the story. He was sympathetic and supportive. For the first time in my memory, I didn't feel as if I were basically a very bad person deep down inside. But, as anyone who has been through the experience of childhood abuse knows, reliving early memories can both begin to free you from guilt while simultaneously eliciting deep emotional distress. Within weeks, my life fell apart, and I felt abandoned by God and by my pastoral counselor, who I felt was not maintaining appropriate boundaries with me.

I began seeing a female psychiatrist, who diagnosed depression. My capacity to study in school was greatly impaired that semester; I couldn't concentrate on the textbooks. I lost all self-esteem, so that even to ask a question in class became a terrifying experience. My psychiatrist offered me antidepressants; but, just as I had rejected drugs for my back injury, I believed I could overcome this on my own. Instead, I walked through each day reliving the traumas, fears, and anxieties of my childhood. I joined support groups; I worked hard in therapy. And I started taking classes in the school's new feminist-liberation theology program. I began slowly to comprehend issues of power and abuse.

In the winter of 1985, my name came up for review before the ordination committee of the Episcopal Church in my effort to become a postulant in the ordination process. I was hopeful that at last I could become an official member of the process, and looked forward to my meeting with the bishop and the standing committee. I was shocked to walk into the committee room, and find that in front of each person was a copy of *Beyond the Body*. About six months previously, my book publisher had contacted me to say they were reissuing my book and that I could make any changes I wanted. My pastoral counselor—whom I had subsequently left, as I just related—had encouraged me to claim my psychic side openly and proudly. So, I had the book republished under my real name. It was on bookstore shelves all over town with my name plastered on it. When I saw the book in the hands of each committee member, I remembered the kind and supportive woman who had sent a copy to the bishop. I knew it was over for me in the Episcopal Church.

And it was. I was questioned intensely about the relationship between psychic phenomena and traditional Christian theology. I had been studying Christian mysticism in school, and did all I could to explain how I saw the connection. But the members did not see it as I did, or at least had concerns about a priest with those views representing the church. I was put on hold indefinitely for postulancy.[2] My abandonment by God was complete. That warm, loving Christ who had ordained me in my dorm room two years before and told me to seek church ordination had left me. Now, I thought, I understand God at last. God is abandonment.

I couldn't tolerate the pain and disillusion of my path to ordained ministry. Clearly, the Episcopal Church wasn't going to ordain me. I probably wasn't really

---

2. I want to make clear that—from the vantage of time and distance—I now know that my experience in the Episcopal Church is not typical of the Church's approach to mysticism. There is a long tradition of mysticism within Anglicanism, and there are many prominent Episcopal lay people and clergy who speak openly and positively about mysticism. Their decision about me probably involved many factors that I know nothing about. Also, the book I had written, on which they based much of their questioning, was focused more on psychic experience than a mystical journey. What is important in relating this episode is its impact on my spiritual journey.

"called." But I was halfway through seminary training, having taken on considerable debt to pay the tuition. It seemed too late to backtrack and get a doctorate in psychology.

I decided to get a Masters Degree in Social Work after seminary so that I could get a job as a social worker. I hated leaving my feminist-liberation studies, however, so decided to work simultaneously on a doctorate of ministry in feminist-liberation theology at the Episcopal Divinity School while also pursuing my M.S.W. at Boston University.

As I completed my seminary studies, there was one brief oasis in my wilderness wandering. My friend from Curriculum Conference days—the holistic-health advocate, Anne—tried to convince me to explore a different church. She had spoken to me for months about Swedenborgianism, which she described as a church that believed in mysticism. As it happened, I had heard of a Swedenborgian minister, a man named Cal Turley, who had been Anne's supervisor on a holistic health field project. Cal, who had died suddenly two years previously, had been a professor at the Swedenborg School of Religion in Newton, Massachusetts. Thus, I found out that there was another seminary just a few miles away from the campus of the Episcopal Divinity School.

That news became a bright spot in my life. Quickly, I made my way to the Swedenborgian seminary and started talking to faculty and students about Emanuel Swedenborg. It was at this time that I first learned that Swedenborg himself had had psychic experiences and wrote numerous books explaining how spirit is in all matter and how the spiritual part of life is its basic reality. I also began attending the Swedenborgian chapel off Harvard Square. I was incredulous to find a real church filled with real people that had a mystical basis to its theology. As I began my studies that fall in social work and in feminist-liberation theology, I managed to find time to slip over to the Swedenborg School of Religion to read and to talk.

It was fortunate that I had one bright spot, as my personal life was becoming a nightmare. My marriage of twenty years was floundering. I had become terrified of my husband's rapidly changing moods and no longer felt safe. Burt, our primary source of income during my student days, began losing jobs, and our income plummeted. My eating disorder—which had first come to my attention in the trance reading back in New Haven— became an oscillating cycle between binging on foods I was allergic to and then fasting for days afterwards.

After sessions with a social worker, my husband and I decided to separate and began mediating a divorce settlement. I got the house (with mortgage) and our cats; he got most of our retirement fund. I was graduating from social work school that year and began working full time as a social worker in New Hampshire, living in the small, rural house with the cats.

The cats kept me company that first bitter winter alone, as I would come home late at night, after working overtime hours for more pay, to find the house miserably cold. I'd try to get a fire going in the old wood stove but it would generally be out again by morning. Burt had always kept the stove going, and I couldn't afford to use the electric heat.

Life was dreary. I liked my clinical work as an addictions specialist and social worker, but I had lost my sense of what my life was all about. I was lonely and grieving for my marriage. I wondered what had happened to my spiritual life. It all seemed like the long-ago past. Now I was a social worker, and I had long since stopped having mystical experiences or feeling God's presence in my life. I had once thought God was calling me to ministry; now God was gone, and I was drifting away from the Episcopal Church.

There was one place where I felt that a reconnection to God could happen: in the Swedenborgian Church. I increasingly felt at home there, finding in Swedenborg a way to understand my New-Age awareness, psychic experiences, mystical experiences, and burgeoning Christianity in a way that blended all the elements together. I felt warmly welcomed in the church and liked the people. I felt that I had a found some elements of what I had loved as a Unitarian-Universalist, in that Swedenborg, like so many mystics, was accepting of all spiritual paths. In addition, his understanding of salvation involved being active in the world, which fit in well with my feminist-liberation theology.

I entered the Swedenborg School of Religion on a part-time basis, working evenings at my social work job to have a day off for taking courses. I studied every weekend. Almost before I realized what I was doing, I found myself in a warm and supportive ordination process. However, I didn't mention my books or my New-Age channeling; that part of me seemed in the distant past since I hadn't given readings or had any psychic experiences for years. But I did talk about how important mysticism was to me, and everyone nodded in total understanding. I felt at home.

I took as many courses at the Swedenborgian seminary as I could while working full time as a social worker. Because I had entered the program with a Masters of Divinity degree, I was required to take only courses that studied Swedenborgian theology and to take part in field experiences. For one of my field experiences, I worked with some people in New Hampshire to start a spiritual growth center we called the Network Center.

In 1990, I found myself scheduled for ordination, with a plan of ministry at the Network Center. I should explain that, as a student at the Newton seminary, I entered into a branch of the Swedenborgian Church known as Convention, the only branch in the United States that ordains women.[3] I wasn't going to get my hopes up about the ordination, however. In my negativity and depression, I figured God would throw a monkey wrench into the works to sabotage it all. In the Convention branch of the Swedenborgian Church, the final vote for ordination takes place before the entire convention, three days before the scheduled event. Despite my certainty that God would find a way to stop this thing from happening, one day I stood before several hundred people who were applauding and giving me a standing ovation—approving me for ordination. I had passed every hurdle in the process.

That was a Friday afternoon in late June of 1990. I was to be ordained the following Sunday morning, July 1. Suddenly, I was terrified. What was I doing? What was I committing myself to? I spent most of those two days in the chapel meditating. There, I again felt Christ in my life—the Christ who had called me seven years ago in a student dorm room. He was still with me! And his love

---

3. There are two other branches of the Church in the United States: the General Church, the seat of which in this country is located in Bryn Athyn, Pennsylvania, where a magnificent Swedenborgian cathedral is the town's focal point; and the Lord's New Church of Nova Hierosolyma.

seemed as strong as ever. Somehow, it seemed that all of my suffering had served a purpose. I committed myself to him all over again. I said that I wanted always to stay in relationship with him and wanted him to bring me whatever life experiences I needed for that to happen. That was a prayer I soon came to regret.

I was frightened as I walked up to the ordination platform that Sunday morning. I had felt Christ again and suspected I was doing something real and permanent in my vows that day. I knelt before a group of people I had selected—laity and ordained—as they laid hands on my head. As I stood up, I knew something had happened, that my very being was changed forever. Energy was pulsing through my body, the same mystical energy I had felt in the Eucharists and my Episcopal Church confirmation. Yet it was more intense than I ever had felt before. I was ecstatic for days.

Although the energy modified, it continued on and off for months. I had never before—and have never since—experienced anything like the joy and ecstasy I felt during that time. Such a shift from the gloom of the past years! Daily life was a moving in and out of trance states. I learned to function well in my job as a social worker, but the mystical energy was never far away.

My wilderness journey was not quite over yet, however. I still had anger at God, which I realized when my mother died in 1991. Mom had become a major source of solace after my divorce and supporter of my spiritual journey. I had finally told her the secret of a childhood trauma I had carried inside for years, and it brought us closer than ever. I was devastated when she was diagnosed with cancer. Death came quickly for her, but I distanced myself from God again, feeling angry and abandoned.

59

Bit by bit, however, the wilderness was becoming tamer. I was doing well as a social worker and was promoted to coordinator of a dual-diagnosis day-treatment program in a mental health center; "dual diagnosis" signifies patients who have mental health problems and an addiction. I loved my work and felt I was becoming a respected professional. I became a Licensed Independent Clinical Social Worker in Massachusetts and a Certified Clinical Social Worker in New Hampshire. I achieved my certificate as a Certified Drug and Alcohol Counselor in New Hampshire. I also continued work on my thesis for my doctorate in ministry at the Episcopal Divinity School. I spent evenings and weekends with the Network Center and used my vacation days for the Swedenborgian Church meetings and conventions.

Laurie, a friend from my Episcopal seminary days, introduced me to a self-help program for people with compulsive eating habits; and, after struggle and denial, I finally admitted that I had eating disorders and got to work on them. I found a therapist who specialized in eating problems and went to a nutritionist. I let my doctor tell me how much I should weigh and gave up making that decision for myself. I went to self-help meetings regularly and used them to make my eating a part of my spiritual life.

For my D.Min. thesis, I began exploring a possible connection between Swedenborgian doctrines and the twelve steps; I learned that Bill Wilson's wife Lois was the granddaughter of a Swedenborgian minister and that Bill and Lois had attended the New York Swedenborgian Church at one point in their married life.

Then, in the spring of 1993, I heard of a job opening at the Swedenborg School of Religion in pastoral care and field education. I considered applying, yet felt that I liked what I was doing and also hated the thought of another change just as I was getting back into balance. I was asked by the school to teach a course on a part-time basis until a permanent replacement could be hired, and I agreed. As I went to the school each week to teach the course, I kept feeling a great pull to be there. I became filled with mystical ecstasy when I entered the school, and it left me when I returned to my social work job. One day, after teaching a class in Religion and Psychology, I sat in the classroom and felt a warm, loving energy around me. Immediately, I thought of Cal Turley, the Swedenborgian professor and mentor of my friend Anne, who had died of a heart attack almost ten years previously. Cal had been professor of pastoral care at the school, the very position that was once again open. I felt I was being encouraged to apply for the position.

As I drove back to New Hampshire, I was confused. Was God giving me a message? I felt it unlikely that I'd be seriously considered for the job, with all the qualified applicants. I liked what I was doing. Yet the energy was compelling; the sense of a dynamic, enthusiastic, warm presence in that room that afternoon had been so strong.

So I applied. As I walked through the months of that process, I came to realize how much I would love teaching at the Swedenborg School of Religion. It would be a wonderful way to integrate my three master's degrees with my Ph.D. in Education and upcoming D.Min. It would let me use my social work training as well as my seminary training. I was amazed to find I was one of two candidates remaining at the end of the selection process.

I was delighted when I got the job offer. I felt that God and I were finally wanting the same thing for my life. I quit my job as a social worker in August of 1993 and in September began my full-time work at Swedenborg School of Religion.

Once again, I was to understand that the process of becoming is never smooth. I soon realized that I felt uneasy teaching students preparing for ministry, when my own relationship with God was still so unclear to me. I asked my friend Anne to recommend a spiritual director, and she suggested a woman she knew at St. John's monastery in Cambridge. As I began work in spiritual direction, it became clear that I still harbored a great deal of anger towards God—anger about childhood trauma, about feeling abandoned by my husband and my first pastoral counselor, about my mother's death, and even about my years of mysticism that were still confusing to me. I began writing long letters to God, expressing my rage. Our relationship became more distant than ever.

In May of 1994, I was ready to be graduated from the Episcopal Divinity School with my Doctorate of Ministry. It had been eight years since I had begun my D.Min. program; I had needed only a few years of classes but had poked along on my thesis for five years until the school told me I had to finish within a year or leave the program. I had written for months, pulling together a feminist theological perspective of the twelve steps of Alcoholics Anonymous and interweaving them with an analysis of Swedenborgian theology. I had loved the work, but I was exhausted. My first year as a faculty member at the Swedenborgian seminary had involved a huge amount of work, as I was still minister at the Network Center and seeing private social work clients.

I sat quietly at the Eucharist at Episcopal Divinity School the night before graduation. It had been a long time since I had been at a campus event. Although fatigued, the beauty of the service perked me up. All of the graduates had marched in procession behind the faculty, all of us robed in academic resplendence. The music was beautiful. Several faculty members together were consecrating the elements. As their eucharistic prayer continued, the energy in the room changed, and once again I felt the presence of Christ with me. I could hear a voice in my head that spoke with the authority of God:

You have now completed the dark night of the soul, and we can enter into union.

I was startled. I thought about all the anger I still had towards God and wondered how a union could be possible.

You have been in a dark night for many years. It has gradually been lifting, and now is the time for it to end. You have completed the work you need to do in that stage. Now we will prepare for a Union deeper and more profound than any you have known before. Many mystics are in a state of anger by the time they finish the dark night, having felt abandoned for so long and having endured many trials. It is normal. Keep expressing the anger and it will pass.

Yes, but . . . .

The voice was gone, and I again became aware of being in the chapel of the Episcopal Divinity School. My row was walking up to receive communion. I followed along, in a confused and puzzled state. As I received the wafer and put it in my mouth, I felt the now familiar, yet long absent blast of love. Tears streamed down my cheeks as I again felt loved and accepted. I felt the presence of Christ, yet it was also clear to me that we didn't have a relationship. And I wasn't certain that I wanted one, with the distrust and anger I had. A kind classmate standing next to me put a tissue in my hand, and I smiled gratefully as I dabbed at my tears. It seemed that, in some way, I was entering a new stage in my spiritual life. I was terrified. I would have been even more frightened if I had realized that, in only six weeks, I would be at our annual gathering of Swedenborgians of Convention consecrating communion when the union experience would happen.

F I V E

Union

July 1, 1994, the final day of convention, dawned muggy and overcast. I was up early to finish my packing. I couldn't focus well, and every task took twice as long as usual. Just two days ago, I had experienced the ecstasy as I administered communion, which I described in the "Prologue."

At the end of our closing service, dozens of Swedenborgians piled into vans that carted our luggage and us to the airport. I thought about the several hours I would have to wait for my flight, but knew I was still ecstatic and much too inner- focused to do any sightseeing.

I couldn't understand this state I was in, but I knew I wasn't functioning well on the physical plane and thought it would be better to find my gate and sit there rather than risk getting lost and confused wandering around.

As I sat down, I became distressingly aware of the

chaotic din around me. Construction was underway, and there seemed to be a half dozen gates all crammed into the same area. A loudspeaker almost continuously announced flights, and people wandered through the seating area looking for concessions or gates. I couldn't imagine a more uncomfortable place to spend several hours waiting for a flight, much less one to meditate in, as I felt drawn to do.

But after settling down, I felt myself drawn into a trance state where everything around me faded away. And I again felt the presence of the Divine as I had felt it while giving communion: pure love was infusing every part of my being. I felt myself drawn back to the energy of Friday's communion. I felt the presence of the Divine in my inner mind in the "intellectual" sense of presence that Teresa talks about. It was as though I had just been married to Christ, and now the honeymoon was beginning and I was starting to know my Beloved. The intensity was such that, at the time of the encounter, everything was clear. All of my questions were answered, and the answers made perfect sense. Even though the clarity faded soon afterward and I know I'll never fully recapture the richness of that time, I will do my best to recreate its essence here.

I felt divine energy becoming present within me as the commotion around me faded into the background. I felt Christ there. My spiritual life had been a roller coaster for several days, and I had a lot of questions. I understood feeling Christ's presence in communion, but in an airport?

No sooner did that thought enter my consciousness than I understood: I understood that the Divine could be experienced in airports as well as on altars.

At that moment, I was filled with pure joy. Truly,

the Divine is everywhere and in all things. I felt as though I were given a blast of pure love, joy, and peace that replaced anything else in its way. Suddenly, the world was transformed. And I *knew*. But knew what? I couldn't say. It can't be said. But I knew what life was all about—it was this pure love. This is what God is; God is pure Love. Everything that is not-love is not-God.

The world was created out of pure Love and out of the purest motives to share love. I remembered that, in my spiritual direction, I had been writing God angry letters about the miserable state of the world. But I now could not remember the feelings that went with the words. For in this moment the world was perfect, not perfect in needing no change, but perfect in that I had come to that given moment doing what I could do to transform the world.

I would learn from that moment and take my learning into the next moment, which would be different from this one yet also perfect in its own way. We cannot stop the transformations until the world and every soul in it reaches the place of pure Love that God occupies.

I had been furious at God for allowing evil in the world; but, in this moment of the mystical encounter, I knew that God was totally trustworthy, incapable of being anything other than love. Evil, I felt, comes from our humanity, not God's divinity. I felt in that moment so intimately intertwined with the Divine that I could see into its essence, its total purity, pure Love. Yet, in that love, I saw commitment to free will. I saw that the only way for humanity to reach the level of the divine love was to live out free will until burning off all our impurities that stood between us and love.

I trusted this Being with all of my heart, soul, and mind. At that moment, I wanted only to live for this divine love, to work in its interests, to be obedient to its will and to serve it within the world. These feelings . . . in this moment . . . this pure joy had to be what was experienced at the moment of physical death when the soul joins God. This had to be the purpose of life and existence, to reach this state and be in this relationship with God.

Whatever I had gone through to reach this point had been worth it. The pain and suffering of the past eleven years had been worthwhile if they had helped prepare me to be in this moment. I would go through many more years of hell on earth to then have another moment of intimacy with the Divine like this one.

Only a week ago, I had been expressing my anger to God for my sufferings of the past years. Now I was giving thanks.

> *Thank you, God, for whatever you have put me through to help prepare me for this moment and this relationship with you. Whatever I had to endure to prepare for this was worth it. Please, help me always to stay in relationship with you. Whatever else I must go through to maintain this relationship, I'll do. I am totally yours, God. Please just guide me in whatever you want me to do and give me the strength to follow your will.*

I felt understanding coming into my mind—not as words, but rather as concepts, as Teresa called hearing with the intellect. They seemed to come from Christ, my Beloved. Although the understanding was received instantaneously, we humans have only words to express our thoughts, so I have translated the concepts into words:

Welcome, my friend, into our new union. For a long time, you have been fighting me, resisting and putting up barriers to my role in your life. I have been working with you for a long time to get you to remove those barriers. At this moment, they do not exist. You are allowing me in, totally and completely. This seems very easy and natural, does it not? Yet you have struggled for years to be able to set aside those barriers. It is the struggle so many are experiencing on your plane. So many pray to me to do something different to make myself known to them. Yet the power is in their hands. They are the ones who have put up the barrier to my presence and they have the power to remove it.

It is a joyful time on my plane when a barrier is lowered, as yours is right now. It is the opening to a new relationship, to one of partnership and working together instead of your fighting me and trying to work on your own. We are united and working as one. It is the state my mystics have sometimes called marriage, because the union is so complete.

Now that you have entered into this union, you will be here forever, unless you willfully walk away from the path. And it will be much harder to do that now with my essence so intertwined with yours.

My reaction to this immediate understanding was itself instantaneous, but, again, I will put it into words:

How could I ever do that? How could anyone ever experience you this way and walk away? I can see how you have transformed lives in an instant—like Saul on the way to Damascus seeing your light and becoming converted. How can you be encountered and still be

resisted? How could I ever again be angry with you or doubt your intentions?

It can happen, my beloved one, and it will happen. You are human and living on the human plane. You cannot live in the intensity of this experience and still function on your plane. You will have to distance from the purity of this moment to live out your life on earth. And as you do so, you will encounter again your angers and your doubts. And this is as it should be. For your angers and doubts are part of the human essence of you and part of the perfection of relating to me. For when you express anger at me, you are not really angry with me. You are angry at the evils and imperfections of humanity and the physical world. Through your anger you come to recognize those imperfections and can work to change them. I am like a mirror, and can reflect back to you all that is unresolved in you and in your world. Bring me all of your fears and doubts and rages—I will shine them back to you through my mirror so that you can learn more about yourself and your fellows and thereby be further transformed towards perfect Love.

You will have anger towards me when you experience the imperfections and evils of your world. I cannot always protect you from the bad intentions of others and the misfortunes of the physical plane; they are neither my choice nor my punishment. They are the price I pay for allowing free will on your plane—for free will is the only way to reach perfection. But I am with you. No matter what happens to you, I am always there. You will have days when you want to distance yourself from me and feel distrustful *or angry. But I will never remove myself from you. I am always here, accepting and loving you for who you are.*

I knew that was true, for I felt complete love and acceptance. I experienced God in that moment as a perfect parent—father and mother—loving me completely and without reservation, knowing all of my faults yet loving me unconditionally anyway. I couldn't believe that I would ever again feel anything but total love, contentment, trust, and serenity.

But the drone of the loudspeaker began to penetrate to the mystical level where my essence had withdrawn—fortunately so, for I heard my flight called. I gathered my things, and groggily made my way towards the gate. Could I still function on the earth? How would life be after this encounter? I knew that, in some way, I would be changed forever.

Despite the ecstasy, I managed to make my plane, arrive in Manchester, New Hampshire, and then find my car at the airport. I had an hour's drive up the interstate and along the rural roads that led to my little house on the edge of the woods. I had just pulled into the long driveway at home, when I heard frenetic meows welcoming me home. My four feline companions never approved of my travels, and they hated the annual church convention that usually took me away for ten straight days. Despite a loving neighbor's tending to them, they made it clear that no one could replace me and I belonged at home. They forgave easily, however, and we snuggled, cuddled, and purred together until bedtime.

The Beloved

In the days that followed, I felt like a woman on her honeymoon. Fortunately, I had planned on several days of rest following convention and had a light schedule planned. The only thing I really wanted to do was sit in my sunny, secluded backyard facing the woods and meditate. Just be. Just be with my Beloved. I would sit back and close my eyes and feel myself filled with divine love. I could feel his presence, totally loving and accepting me. I felt myself totally in love with this divine being, wanting only to be with him every moment and wanting to shut out the world so that we could be alone in our intimacy.

My cats heartily approved of my sitting for hours in the backyard. They seemed proud of me for finally "getting" what life was all about. For me, meditating for hours was a new way to have a vacation. Normally, these times were filled with reading mystery books or watching videos, going to movies and plays, socializing with friends. I knew I couldn't focus enough to watch a movie or read a book, and I didn't want to do anything that would distract me from time with my Beloved.

The only reading I could do—and felt drawn to do—was poetry of the mystics. I needed to be reassured that I was not the only one to have fallen in love with Spirit.

My mystics did not let me down. I read their lines over and over again between long periods of meditation.

St. Teresa also wrote poetry, and I reread my favorite verse of hers describing what happened after she gave herself to divine love:

> And lo! My lot so changed is
> That my Beloved One is mine
> And I at last am surely His.[1]

St. John was another of my favorites and one of the most explicit about having romantic encounters with his spirit Beloved:

> Oh night that joined the lover
> To the beloved bride,
> Transfiguring them each into the other.[2]

I was convinced that it was not just Christian mystics who had experiences this union with a Beloved. Thus, I read Krishnamurti:

---

1. Teresa of Avila, "My Beloved One is Mine," in Shelley Gross, ed., *The Mystic in Love: A Treasury of World Mystical Poetry* (New York: Bantam., 1976), 160.
2. St. John of the Cross, "Songs of the Soul in Rapture," in *The Mystic in Love*, 119–120.

As two mountain streams meet . . .
Joyous in their exultation,
So have I met Thee, O my Beloved.[3]

Some of the romantic concepts were more medieval and had more traditional sex roles than I was
comfortable with or was finding in my own encounters.
But I felt convinced that, centuries apart, we were sharing a commonality of experience.

I wondered about where the mystics of today are?
Are there mystics around today experiencing mystical
marriage? I remembered a mystic friend Jim from my
days at Episcopal Divinity School. If anyone fit my im-
pression of modern mystic it was he, so I called him.

The conversation that followed was exciting to me,
comforting and assuring that I was indeed having true,
positive mystical experiences. Jim had known of
Swedenborg for a long time and admired him greatly;
Jim even knew other Swedenborgians.

In a lengthy telephone conversation, I filled Jim in
on my past and present spiritual experiences. He ex-
pressed surprise that I had spent so much time in the
"dark night," given my past studies in psychology and
my extended support group. He explained that he had
experienced union two years ago, and it was a profound
experience.

But one of the most interesting questions Jim
raised was that of authenticity. He gently asked me if I
had sought psychiatric help—only because some aspects
of psychosis and bipolar disorder simulate the ecstatic

3. Krishnamurti, "My Beloved and I Are One," in *The Mystic in
Love*, 150.

experience. Indeed, he mentioned that mysticism and mental illness often overlap, and that the mentally ill mystic can have some very dangerous experiences. Of course, I had sought therapy at one point and had been working on various personal issues throughout my spiritual journey; Jim thought that such a course was helpful in making sure that the experiences were authentic.

Jim's own betrothal experience was a remarkable one. In the 1970s, Jim had been a communist and an atheist, and spent a good deal of his time in radical activities. One day he had a strange compulsion to stop in a church and rest. He went in, closed his eyes, and cleared his mind of his worries. When he opened his eyes, he saw Jesus standing before him. Jim described the figure as an actual man, not an image or mirage, but a solid figure standing before him. The Jesus who appeared to Jim wasn't the white-skinned, blue-eyed man that this communist might disdain, but a man with brown skin and dark eyes, a "third-world" man. His hands were those of a working man, rough and weathered.

Jim, as you might imagine, panicked; he immediately thought that he was having an acid flashback. After trying to do all the things he knew to clear his head, he opened his eyes again—and there, holding his ground, was Jesus.

"I want you to be a priest," the man said.

"I'm not a Christian," Jim responded.

"You have to decide *now*," Jesus said.

Jim thought about this ultimatum for a while that evening in the church; but, when he meditated on the figure before him, he knew he had to capitulate. His answer was, "I am yours, Lord. Do with me as you will."

When Jim finished uttering these words, Jesus approached him and put his hands over Jim's heart. He felt an incredible surge of loving energy jolt through his body. Jim believes that this gesture signified that he would always feel Jesus' presence inside him, a promise that he would never be alone.

As you might expect, given Jim's past, many of his friends did not believe in his conversion. He himself spent a long time coming to terms with his experiences. One man, an Episcopal priest, believed Jim's story and encouraged him to put his new love into action. Jim worked with the homeless in the priest's parish for two years. He shared his story with many people, as he eventually worked his way to ordination as an Episcopal priest.

Jim regards that encounter with Jesus as a betrothal. His own long journey after that fateful evening in the church included a two-year-long "dark night." But, then, he emerged from the suffering into union. Since that time, he has explored meditation with Buddhists.

As you can imagine, Jim's story was an affirmation of my own experience. He encouraged me to trust my feelings, to enter into the mystical relationship with resolve. He stressed that the relationship was one of ongoing purification, not static and not always ecstatic. Rather, all unresolved personal issues will come to the surface and will have to be worked on. He also stressed that I shouldn't ignore my physical needs or my professional work. It seems that, to Jim, a real mystic was a person engaged in this world.

Now I had to decide whether to continue the honeymoon here at home or at a convent/retreat center in Biddeford, Maine. I had been invited to join this retreat some months ago by friends who are Sisters of Mercy. I had become interested in the Sisters when I realized that many of them were social activists and involved in many of the feminist activities in New Hampshire. I admired the support and solidarity in this group of women and the way in which they combined spirituality with social involvement. I was getting to know many of them and contemplating becoming an associate member of the order.

I felt drawn to, and uneasy about, being around nuns that week. I saw them as having made a commitment to be married to Christ, and having taken a public vow of that commitment. I felt married to Christ in the mystical sense; but, if I started talking about that, it would sound bizarre to most people and probably offensive to nuns who went through years of postulancy, novitiate, and temporary vows before making that commitment.

I thought for a long time about my conversation with Jim. His entreaty not to neglect the outer world won the day. I was soon on my way to the retreat in Maine.

The retreat in Biddeford, Maine, with the Sisters of Mercy was as rewarding as I had expected it to be. We had a terrific two-day workshop on Native American spirituality, followed by a day of silence.

For many of the women there, this was a reunion. Some of them saw each other only at this annual retreat. Some hadn't seen each other for years—since they had been novices together. Those who were only a few years older than I had entered convents that were rigid and structured, and they had worn traditional habits for their first few years. Then Vatican II had come along, and, suddenly, everything changed. Almost overnight, nuns were giving up wearing habits for street clothes and were moving out of convents to apartments. Many of the women had "band" reunions that week, a reunion of those who had entered the novitiate together.

Having no long-term bonds with the others, I spent time alone on the beach. I drifted in and out of trance; in and out of meditation. I missed lunch and was later told that I had looked so peaceful no one wanted to disturb me.

While lying on the beach, I was able to feel the presence of my Beloved with my inner spirit, the "intellectual" type of vision that Teresa describes. I sunk into blissful oblivion, as ecstatic words of poetry drifted into my mind:

> *I am a drop of water and*
> *You are the sea.*
> *I am a grain of sand and*
> *You are the beach.*
>
> *I am a cloud and*
> *You are the sky.*
>
> *I am a sunbeam;*
> *You are the sun.*
>
> *We are one, my Beloved*
> *We are one.*
>
> *I am Thee*
> *Thou art me.*
>
> *Together we will be*
> *For eternity.*

I felt the bliss. Yet I also realized how new and strange this relationship was for me. I tried to form the words to express this to my Beloved:

78

I feel I've surrendered to you and your Love. A couple of weeks ago, I would have said that in no way would I ever surrender to anyone—especially a male. I'm a feminist; women have been oppressed for eons by men, and we're still expected to surrender to them. I don't even believe in surrender to God—who for me is both male and female. I've never really surrendered to a Higher Power, or considered it necessary. Yet, with the intensity of the experiences you've brought me, I feel as if I've completely surrendered myself and my life to you.

I couldn't actually hear words in response, but I sensed concepts and understandings in my mind. Their translation into words is something like:

I'm not a male. I'm both genders or, more accurately, neither gender. I'm Spirit. You haven't surrendered to a male; you've surrendered to the Spirit of Love.

Still, I couldn't think about surrender without considering hierarchies and oppression. Again I felt understanding coming to mind.

In heaven, there are hierarchies, but these are based on one's love and purity. There's no way to fake the level of love one has achieved. So you can always trust those above you in the heavenly hierarchy to be more advanced in love and purity than you and to be able to help you get to the next level. And as you develop these qualities more deeply, you advance on the hierarchy and help those below you to move up. It's a perfect system. Unfortunately, like many of the heavenly realities, this one has been corrupted on earth by power. Those more advanced on the

79

earthly hierarchies are not necessarily wiser or more loving. Actually, people in authority often seek power to oppress others with it. A beautiful concept from heaven, which helps people give and receive guidance along their path of love, is corrupted and used to abuse people on earth.

I stared at the waves crashing gently on the sandy beach, with the sun beating down overhead. It was an exquisite day. How could I make sense of what I was experiencing inside myself? I didn't have trouble believing my Beloved was Jesus Christ—or God or Love—because what I felt was so profound. I thought of Swedenborg's term "the Lord" to describe the one God, which described what I felt. Yet, this relationship with the Divine seemed so intimate and casual. "The Lord" was always a concept to me, one that seemed so distant. This presence felt close, warm and personal. I thought about the idea of "mystical marriage" and realized that I did indeed feel married and that my spouse was divine yet was also warm and personal—human, in a way. I felt I was encountering the human dimension of the Divine. Wasn't that what the life of Jesus was all about—a chance to know the human part of God that we could relate to?

The peace and quiet of the day penetrated deep into my soul. Life was perfect in that moment on the beach. I wanted it to go on forever. I cried out to the presence I felt, "Why must this ever end? Can't I spend my life on a beach basking in my love for You?"

Concepts crystallized in my mind:

You're not called to a beach or to a secluded convent. You're called into the world. That's what the Incarnation was all about: taking the self into the world to be of service. But you won't be alone.

Those thoughts left me frightened. How could I function in the world after this intense mystical encounter? How could I live day by day again after this intimate glimpse of the Divine? I knew that, at the very least, I would keep this experience a secret. How could I ever share with anyone what this "mystical marriage" was like? There were no words. When I had written about my psychic experiences years ago, I was deterred in seeking an Episcopal postulancy. What could I lose as a Swedenborgian minister if I ever admitted to anyone what was happening in the depths of my being? What I felt in response was terrifying: I felt that I was being called back into living my daily routine *and* into finding a way to integrate my mysticism with my life. I also had to do all this in a way that allowed sharing and openness of my spirituality, rather than secrecy. I wondered if I really had surrendered to the Lord after all. I just wanted to run away.

Call

The final days of the summer of 1994 melded together in a blur of activity. I spent two weeks at the
Fryeburg New Church Assembly, our Swedenborgian
camp in Maine. My time there was filled with the usual
peace and tranquility of wooded community life, yet it
was also hectic as I had agreed to give four lectures. I
now found myself having to function in the world again
after weeks of mystical bliss. It was a bumpy return. I
wasn't even current with world or national news. The
last thing I remembered seeing on television, toward the
end of June, was O. J. Simpson's leading the police on a
long chase late one Friday night. My television hadn't
been on since then. "Reading" had become glancing at
the headlines of the daily newspaper and staring at the
pictures in *Time* and *Newsweek*. I was reasonably certain
that a third world war hadn't started. And I had a vague
sense that O. J. had become big news. But beyond that,

I was ignorant. The news inside of me seemed so much more compelling than anything else for so long.

The honeymoon was over, and I was settling into married life. It was not an easy adjustment. Some days I felt warmth and bliss in my relationship; at other times, I experienced an exacting, demanding spouse. As the dark-green leaves of August started showing splashes of orange, red, and yellow, I fought regularly with my Beloved over whether or not I would share anything about our relationship.

In my journal, I wrote:

> I'm terrified to talk about my experiences. I'm a private person, and mystics have been attacked throughout history. I can't share my spiritual life with others. I'd at least get criticized and maybe even hurt in some way. You understand, don't you, Lord, that that's not something I can do.
>
> I can't understand why are you asking me to do it? I've got a happy life, with a job I love. Why should I take the risks involved in getting closer to you? You seem to make demands on me that could make my life much less tranquil! Why would I want to tell anyone about my experiences with you? Why would I want to write about my mysticism? These are controversial topics, and I don't like stirring up problems. Why should I bother doing any of it?

As I wrote, I had an image of Jesus on the cross. I thought about how his earthly mission had involved following his path, even when it led to great pain and death. How could I live in fear when he had done so much?

It occurred to me that following a call often involves some risk in not knowing how things will turn out. It means a willingness to do something without a guarantee in advance that there will be no unpleasant consequences. A call, I realized, involves working toward a higher purpose than what we can see right in front of us. That must be what faith is all about.

I struggled to integrate the mysticism in my life. After those profound, intense encounters of the summer, I was back in a life where I had to pay bills, maintain my car, and live out a regular life. Why, I wondered, did I have to be plagued with mystical experiences that seemed to serve no purpose? Perhaps, I thought, if I could mystically know before an accident or car breakdown was to happen I could be spared a great deal of life's pain. It seemed that, if I had to live in a mystical marriage, then my Beloved should use his powers to protect me from being hurt on the earthly plane.

In response to those thoughts, I found many ideas flowing into my head:

> *The physical plane exists for a reason; it provides an arena for spiritual growth—spiritual growth within physical reality. It only works if you walk the path of the physical, accepting its limitations and pains as well as its joys. If you try to escape the consequences of the physical, then the purpose is defeated. If God intervened to warn people before accidents or car breakdowns, then no one would ever wear seat belts or service their cars—or work to create a world with a safer and cleaner mode of transportation.*

I cried as I absorbed those words, saying in my mind to my Beloved:

> *I guess I thought that somehow my mysticism would protect me from hurt on this plane.*

In response, again I could sense concepts in my mind:

It doesn't. When you do get hurt, you feel that God has abandoned you and you withdraw. You're not alone in that, you know. So many people want the Divine to suspend the physical laws in their lives and protect them from the pains of the earth. And there are a great many who live lives of buried rage against God because of the pains they endure. God loves the Earth and its people and is committed to letting everyone live out their free will.

All this just makes me feel awfully vulnerable living on Earth. I guess I thought being married to you might give me some extra protection.

You need to work to change your world. You deserve a world where people don't get slaughtered on the highways or die from cancer. Your world can be changed, but only by people working on the physical plane to change the physical circumstances—not by people counting on the mystical world to suspend the physical laws for their convenience.

It all made sense, of course. But for the first time since my mystical marriage had begun, I felt terribly alone and vulnerable. I really had thought that my Beloved would protect me in some way. But why should I be protected any more than anyone else? Clearly, I had a much bigger ego than I had ever realized.

Over the next few days, I thought a lot about what my Beloved seemed to be saying to me. I was hearing about a way of life that involved taking risks and accepting the consequences, about following a call even if it would involve pain. I was hearing that pain was part of our life on the physical plane and would continue to be so, although we all could work on the earth to alleviate our circumstances.

I suspected that my Beloved was, at heart, a social activist, and I, too, would have to become more involved in working to change the world if I were to take the words seriously. I decided to join the political and legislative action committees of the New Hampshire social workers to become more involved in the issues of my state.

I realized that I only felt comfortable sharing my spiritual life with a select few who might understand. I had shared my experiences of the summer only with Jim. My spiritual director from St. John's Monastery was back now from a summer break, and it was time to start talking about my Beloved.

It was now the end of September 1994. I drove to St. John's Monastery in Cambridge; the monastery was a picture of tranquility with its medieval stone structure. It all seemed like a sea of tranquility in the midst of hectic Cambridge.

I fixed a cup of tea in the waiting area, and sat down. My spiritual director had been away all summer, and now I needed to update her about all of the changes in my spiritual life.

"Hi, nice to see you again!" She greeted me with her usual warmth and took me down the narrow stairway to her small but cozy office with two comfortable chairs, a desk piled high with papers, and bookshelves piled with books.

I brought her up to date on my summer adventures, and she asked me how I was doing with my anger at God.

I was thoughtful for a few minutes. "I haven't

thought of that in those terms, but, you know, I think I am angry. I think I'm starting to access my rage again. It disappeared when the mysticism hit last summer, but it's never been resolved. I still have the same questions about why this stuff is dumped on me. I never asked for mystical experiences; I don't want to write or talk about them. During the ecstasy I felt willing to make any commitment to serve God. And I'm still willing to do almost anything to serve. But being in constant relationship with the Lord is one of the hardest and most agonizing things I could be asked to do. He keeps pointing out to me the areas in which I need to grow. He's asking me to share my mysticism with others. Why does God pick the hardest possible things to ask?"

"You know," she said, reaching for a Bible on her shelf, "you're not the first one to have that kind of reaction to a call from God. Look at what it was like for the prophets. Listen to this from Isaiah [6:5–8], when he is having this overwhelming vision of God."

> "Woe is me, for I am undone!
> Because I am a man of unclean lips,
> And I will dwell in the midst of a people of
>   unclean lips;
> For my eyes have seen the King,
> The Lord of hosts."

> Then one of the seraphim flew to me, having in his hand a live coal, which he had taken with the tongs from the alter.

> And he touched my mouth with it, and said:

> "Behold, this has touched your lips;
> Your iniquity is taken away,
> And your sin purged.

Also I heard the voice of the Lord, saying:

"Whom shall I send,
And who will go for Us?'

Then I said, "Here am I! Send me."

"It's often just the last part that's quoted, where he offers to go," my spiritual director said. "But look what he had just been through! He had this incredible vision followed by having his lips touched with a hot coal. How much free will did he really have in that moment? Could he have said 'no' then? He must have been fairly traumatized by it all."

When I thought about it, I realized that I too had always seen Isaiah as a model of willingness to answer a call. My director explained that, indeed, most of the prophets struggled with their calls to the extent that she often wondered how freely chosen their consent was. She assured me that my struggle sounded similar.

I felt tears in my eyes. It was a relief to hear someone question the aspect of free will. After all, I didn't choose the mystical experiences. But having had them, it felt impossible to reject them, to say "No!" You can't say "no" in the midst of an experience where you're feeling filled up with and surrounded by God's love.

My spiritual director urged me to read the words of the prophets in the Hebrew Bible to find solidarity with their struggle and to come to terms with my own.

We set an appointment for another two weeks, and I left in a thoughtful mood. As I made my way down the long corridors out to the parking lot, I became aware that my rage was starting to return. What right did God have to impose all these demands on my life? I was an ordained minister teaching in a seminary. In addition to my full-time teaching job, I conducted Sunday services each week, performed weddings and funerals, and put countless hours into the Network Center, a spiritual growth center in New Hampshire. What more could God ask of me? I had responded five years ago to a call of ordination and was doing what I believed to be God's will. Now, I also had to deal with my mystical experiences. I felt furious about this intrusion into my life. It was time to read the prophets.

That evening I picked up my Bible. I reread the verses from Isaiah that my spiritual director had read to me that afternoon, reflecting that, indeed, it must have been traumatizing to have your lips touched with a hot coal in the midst of mystical encounter with the Divine. What else could one say but "Here I am, Lord, send me"?

I turned next to Jeremiah to look up the story of his call. I found it in the first chapter (Jeremiah 1: 4–10).

> Now the word of the Lord came to me, saying,
> "Before I formed you in the womb I knew you.
> And before you were born I sanctified you;
> I ordained you a prophet to the nations."

Jeremiah responded,

> "Ah, Lord God!
> Behold, I cannot speak, for I am a youth."

The Lord, however, did not accept that excuse, saying,

> "Do not say, 'I am a youth';
> For you shall go to all to whom I send you,
> And whatever I command you, you shall speak.
> Do not be afraid of their faces,
> for I am with you to deliver you."

Then, as in the case of Isaiah, the Lord touched Jeremiah's mouth, although this time not with a hot coal. The Lord said,

> "Behold, I have put My words in your mouth.
> See, I have this day set you over the nations
> and over the kingdoms,
> To root out and to pull down,
> To destroy and to throw down,
> To build and to plant."

How must that have felt? I wondered. A young man living a fairly ordinary life has a profound experience, with a voice claiming to have known him since before his birth. His protest that he is too young is ignored. And then God says "You must go to everyone I send you to and say whatever I command you." Clearly, God is not saying: "Here's an opportunity, Jeremiah, to which you can say 'yes' or 'no.' Either is fine. It's your choice." Instead, God is saying, "You will!" Pretty powerful stuff to encounter in one's youth. Could Jeremiah possibly have said "no?" Was rejection even an option?

I read further to find out more about how Jeremiah really felt about his call and found the following in chapter 20: 7–9:

> "O Lord, you induced me, and I was persuaded;
> You are stronger than I, and have prevailed.
> I am in derision daily;
> Everyone mocks me.
> For when I spoke, I cried out,
> I shouted, "Violence and plunder!"
> Because the word of the Lord was made to me
> A reproach and a derision daily.
> Then I said, "I will not make mention of Him,
> Nor speak anymore in His name."

But His word was in my heart like a burning fire
Shut up in my bones:
I was weary of holding it back,
And I could not.

I felt empathy with the Jeremiah of those verses. He was saying he never felt the call was a totally free choice; it had resulted from overpowering strength. And in living out the call, he met ridicule and mockery from others. Yet if he decided to quit doing the Lord's will, he was miserable with a burning fire in his heart that he could not hold in. Some free choice! Although my mystical experiences seemed modern, updated, and refined for a twentieth-century woman, there seemed to be a lot of ways in which the divine encounter really hadn't changed since the days of the prophets. I thought how good it felt to have found a friend in a prophet.

Understanding

Of course, even though I became acquainted with the experiences of others, I was still far away from complete understanding and acceptance of my own experiences. The fall of 1994 was a period of intense introspection and questioning, as my journal entries from that period attest:

> Dear Lord, I know what you are asking of me, to commit myself to our relationship—or more accurately to acknowledge and accept the relationship that already exist, to stop fighting you and start working with you. I feel that, ultimately, I really have no choice. I do not think it possible to say "no" to you. But it is important to me that you understand all that I am feeling about this.
>
> I am weary after a busy week of serving you in so many ways. This weekend, I conducted a funeral and had to drive into Massachusetts on both

Saturday and Sunday for the service and then the burial. I had spent hours last week working with the family on writing the service. It was a lot of work, and I wondered why I was doing it. But as I stood in front of that room full of people in the funeral home, seeing wet eyes and sorrowful expressions and I talked about eternal life, I knew I was doing what I love. I love being a minister. I love being *your* minister. It is a part of me. To be fully me, I must be your minister.

It's more than that, though. After the burial yesterday, I came home and went out to my garden. This is my favorite time of year in New Hampshire, with the glorious fall colors and the final warm sunny days of the season. I picked the last of the squash and planted more catnip for a fresh spring supplies for my cats. And as I dug there in my organic raised beds feeling the warmth of the sun on my face, I knew that you have become a part of me. And I have become a part of you. When this "mystical marriage" happened, something profound changed inside. Now when I try to fight *you*, I'm also fighting *me*. I'm fighting the essence of who I am. For in some mysterious way, my very essence is now tied up with you. I cannot be *me* any more without also being in relationship with you. I love you. Sometimes I am so angry at you. Yet I also am in love with you. I can't change that feeling or make it go away. I am in love, and I cannot walk away from you.

Do you really understand how this leaves me feeling angry, for it seems that I have no free will? Do you really care how it feels to get a call from you? Do you understand the power and the pain that come along with your calls?

Recently, I saw a magazine article on the subject

93

of the "call." It sent me back to my Bible. It says in Isaiah 55:3, "Incline your ear, and come to me: listen, so that you may live. I will make with you an everlasting covenant." This sounds so appealing. Yet, so often we try to walk away from making covenants with you.

I'm starting to understand better what it is you are calling me to do. You are calling me to *be*. I was reading about the Rule of St. Benedict written in sixth-century Italy. St. Benedict saw us as being called into relationship with the Divine. And it is a relationship that *you* initiate.

This is what you have been saying to me, Lord—that *you* are calling me into relationship. Do you have any idea how painful that is for me? I have had so many bad relationships in my life. It's hard to envision one that is healthy. It's especially hard since I think of you as having so much power and of me as having so little.

I'm afraid of your power, Lord; it terrifies me. I've been hurt by the power held by people. How do I know I won't be hurt by you?

I saw my spiritual director last week and told her I did not understand how you could expect me to be comfortable in a relationship with you given my past. And she said: "The one part of your statement I'd like to highlight is the idea of being comfortable in a relationship with God. It's not, inherently, a comfortable relationship."

She is right. You are not all that comfortable to be around; you keep reminding me of my higher purposes. I am quite content with how my life is set up right now. You are coming to a content person and asking for risk and change. I am happy as things are *now*. I don't see how changes will make me any happier, but I do see how they could make my life less secure. Yet I realize that my comfort, happiness, and security are not high on your list of goals for me. And that's very scary. You keep talking about service, and I know you consider that more important than comfort. I am frightened of being in relationship with you!

Writing out my fears in a letter to God seemed to help. By putting them into words, I could begin to recognize the fears that gripped me and see how they came from my past. I was taking my unresolved issues from my personal relationships and bringing them into my relationship with the Lord.

I was comforted by turning to Swedenborg. In one of his "memorable relations," or visits to the higher plane, he had a conversation with spirits about free will. He recorded in *True Christian Religion*, section 74:3:

> For if God should violate man's freedom of will, man's dwelling place in God would be destroyed, and there would remain only God's dwelling place in man; which dwelling place is in all who are on earth and who are in the heavens, and even in those who are in the hells; and this is the source of their power, their will, and their understanding. . . . God does not forsake [anyone], but they forsake God.

And where, in fact, was my free will? I had been feeling that my life was out of control with my mystical experiences. I didn't know when they would come or how long they would last. I felt the Lord was inviting me into a deeper, more intimate relationship. Yet, could I say "no"? Did I have the free will to push God away?

I turned again to Swedenborg, who reminded me of the Gospel of John 15: 4,5:[1]

> Abide in me as I abide in you. Just as the branch cannot bear fruit by itself unless it abides in the vine, neither can you unless you abide in me. I am the vine, you are the branches. Those who abide in me and I in them bear much fruit, because apart from me you can do nothing.

> From these plain statements it is clear that the conjunction of the Lord and man is reciprocal; and because it is reciprocal it necessarily follows that man ought to conjoin himself to the Lord, in order that the Lord may conjoin himself to man; and that otherwise conjunction is not effected, but withdrawal and a consequent separation, yet not on the Lord's part, but on man's part. In order that such reciprocal conjunction may exist, there is granted to man freedom of choice, giving him the ability to walk in the way to heaven or in the way to hell.

So I was free to withdraw from the Lord *or* to move closer to conjunction. I hadn't chosen how the Lord would come to me, but I could choose how I would go to the Lord.

Still, everything, I realized, comes from God, even my capacity to choose to relate to the Divine. Further on in the same section of *True Christian Religion*, Swedenborg wrote the following:

---

1. In *True Christian Religion*, section 371:2, Swedenborg wrote about this passage from John, as well as about several other biblical passages.

For the Lord acts, and from him man receives action, and operates as if of himself . . . . This op-
eration of man from the Lord is imputed to [man]
as his own, because he is held constantly by the
Lord in freedom of choice. . . . This freedom the
Lord gives to man to enable him to conjoin himself reciprocally with the Lord, and by conjunction be gifted with eternal life and blessedness,
since this, without reciprocal conjunction, would
not be possible.

So God gave me even the capacity to choose; and
by making a choice, I was using the Lord's gift.

I remembered all of the reasons I had rejected
Christianity years ago and then had not wanted to return to it. I resented the emphasis on self-negation and
self-denial. I saw it as a way of life that society pushed on
women and on racial and class minorities as part of oppression. I saw it as something that happened to code-
pendents, to victims of childhood abuse. I saw it as
unhealthy and as something to be resisted. My healing
process throughout the wilderness wandering had been
one of affirming myself, claiming my space in the world,
and validating my needs. It took a long time even to
identify my needs and a much longer time to claim a
right to have them met. Through years of therapy and
struggle, I had found myself and had earned a healthy
self-esteem and self-respect. Was God now asking of me
that I return to a state of codependency and low self-esteem? I could not—and would not—do that.

On the other hand, I remembered my mystic
friend Jim's saying that everything unresolved in me
would come to the surface during union. Could it be
that as the Lord moved in more closely to me, there was

a bright divine light shining that highlighted every de-
fect of mine that needed my attention?

One morning, en route to work, I took the bus in
to South Station in Boston, where I walked two blocks
to catch a city bus to Newton. I was dropped off about
half a mile from the school and walked the distance car-
rying all that I needed for the day in my backpack. I was
feeling more rested and felt as though God were with
me, as though I could hear a voice, as these ideas flowed
into my mind:

> *To be in relationship with divine love, you have
> to shed your own ego. Not your self— your being,
> your essence, your personality. These are the
> things you gained in your healing process
> through the wilderness. Now that you have a
> healthy self-esteem, you're ready to give up the
> selfishness that prevents you from being totally
> present in the world in a state of love. Everyone
> on a spiritual path has to face this sooner or
> later. For you, the time is now.*

I'd never considered myself a particularly selfish
person. I worked as a minister, teacher, and social
worker. I volunteered my time, gave money to charity.
So where was all this selfishness? I didn't understand.

> *Fear. Fear will bring you back to selfishness. It
> makes you hesitate to express all that is within
> and to follow as you are guided. With fear, the
> ego can stand in the way of a relationship with
> the Divine.*

It kept coming back to that. To being more open,
more trusting, more willing to be in relationship with the
Lord. I knew I was struggling to understand something

intellectually that could only be experienced. Yet, my moments of mystical ecstasy were now rare. How could I relate to the Divine in my daily life?

As I asked the question, I felt answers moving through my consciousness:

> *The traditional spiritual disciplines: prayer, scripture reading, meditation, yoga, journal writing. They have worked for many throughout history.*

Yes, of course. I had been letting my disciplines slip. With an occasional experience of ecstasy, it seemed easy to just drift along until another mystical moment hit my life. But the mystics I had read had all emphasized the daily disciplines. I needed to do that, too.

At that point, I was approaching the school, and I walked in for a quiet day of paperwork as well as our usual chapel debriefings. Every Friday, a faculty member met with each student who had done a school chapel service that week to assess and process it. It was a good experience for faculty as well as students, and I valued that we had time built into our schedule for it.

I began my spiritual disciplines the next day. As I wrote in my journal that night, I became humbled at the realization of how focused on myself I was all day long. I wrote down all of the times I withheld something or ex-aggerated something out of fear of what others would think. I noticed how often I was oblivious to the needs of others because of preoccupation with my own inner life. I noted the times I felt judgmental towards another person.

I realized that my whole way of interfacing with God was with the passivity of meditation. I hardly ever prayed. Prayer seemed too traditional, too Christian to me, and meditation was "New Age" and Eastern. Yet suddenly I needed prayer—and in the most traditional and Christian of styles. I knelt by the side of my bed, with my hands together. "Dear God," I prayed, "please help me with this. I see now what I need. I need to let go of running my life from my ego. I need to turn that over to you. I have to learn what it means to live a life of service. I have to learn how to open to you, to listen to you, and to be willing to follow your will. Please help me learn to do this." I felt surrounded by warmth and love and knew my prayer was heard. And with a pang of fear, I suspected my prayer would also be answered.

On the following Sunday, I met as usual with the Celestial Circle, our Sunday-morning worship group in Concord, New Hampshire. I talked about the meaning of "call" in our lives. We meditated on the subject, and all of us felt some experience of surrender to a higher will.

After our worship, I ate my lunch on the front steps of the vine-covered brick building where we rented space, watching the Main Street activity on a gorgeous fall day. Then I made my way to the other end of Main Street to join the march for a Martin Luther King holiday in New Hampshire. I was pleased to see a contingent from the Sisters of Mercy there and marched with them behind their banner. I knew I had to take my spirituality into the world for it to have meaning. That is what God was calling me to do, and I had to respond.

REFLECTIONS ON THE PAST
Crosses

I think of this time as my "cross" period, and the symbol does indeed have special significance. Not only was it a period of my return to Christianity, but it was also a time when I learned to carry the cross of mysticism. In some ways, it was an actual death to the person I was before; it also involved a rebirth—or at least, the first stage of a rebirth—to a new understanding of life in general and of my life in particular. I saw now—clearly, although none too happily—that we are each called to a mission, that we each have a special relationship with the Divine.

My own call, although not clearly defined at that time (and still evolving at this) was to accept my mystical spirituality and let it be the basis for my relationship with God and the context for my relationship with others. This is a part of me, of my essence; there is no running away from it. Another innate part of me was a call to social action. I was working toward coalescing the two in my roles as minister, teacher, and social worker. It did seem to me, however, that part of my call was to speak out, not be secretive about my mysticism or silent about the need for change in society.

The change over this ten-year period was remarkable. I had gone from a "wilderness wandering" to a real acceptance of my situation and had come to a point at which I knew I had to go forward. Perhaps my final destination was not yet obvious—can I say even now that it is?—but I at least knew that I was on a path that would lead me to my home, the place that God intended me to be.

NEW-AGE PERSPECTIVES

I have found little New-Age literature to help me understand wilderness wandering. Often, New Agers will see this period as a breakdown of the seeker's faith. The New Age sometimes gets mired in its roots, some of which go back to Norman Vincent Peale's ideas of positive thinking.[1] There is, at times, a tendency to believe that good things happen to those who live in faith and

1. I have written more about the background of the New Age, as I see it, in *Wings and Roots: The New Age and Emanuel Swedenborg in Dialog* (San Francisco: J. Appleseed, 1999). See also David Spangler, *Everyday Miracles: The Inner Art of Manifestation* (New York: Bantam Books, 1996), 22.

bad things happen to those who don't. Although this attitude can liberate our ability to visualize and affirm, it can also leave us with guilt if events are not going well. When my mom was dying of cancer, she read books about healing and felt there had to be something wrong with her faith if she wasn't healed by a miracle. If she continued to believe, she thought, surely God would heal her. Some of this attitude, of course, involves the stages of denial experienced by a dying person. Some of it, however, came from the material she read which suggested that true faith always heals.

Most mystical traditions acknowledge suffering and hardship and tend to see them as part of the spiritual journey. The New Age is not, in itself, a spiritual tradition, but rather a blending of many different traditions. Its strength is in the variety it honors; its weakness is in having a superficial grasp of many paths, without necessarily following any of them to their depth. I feel that the New Age opened me to spiritual growth in a way no religion could have. Yet, I also felt abandoned by the New Age when I entered the wilderness, as I could find no signposts to guide me. Only by going deeply into the literature of mysticism could I understand.

I explored a range of modern spiritual literature to understand my relationship with the Divine and how God had become Beloved to me. The material I consulted is not all technically "New Age," but is part of the literature being consulted by many of today's spiritual seekers. I found myself perusing the works of Jungian James Hillman and writers influenced by him, such as Thomas Moore and Jean Houston.

I particularly valued attending a workshop given by JEAN HOUSTON and then reading her book *The Search for the Beloved: Journeys in Mythology and Sacred Psychology*, in which she talks of using all of one's wounds and betrayals to bring about wholeness.[2] Houston used the term "Entelechy Self" to describe the essence of self, the part of one's being that is closest to God. It is, I think, what I have called Higher Self or Higher Power. Houston says this Entelechy Self can be experienced as a separate personality who is the Beloved of one's soul. She revives a term that James Hillman utilized: *pothos*. The term dates back to ancient Greece and refers to deep memory of the human-divine union. This could certainly be a description of my relationship to my Beloved.

Another helpful resource I found was *The Bond with the Beloved* by Sufi LLEWELLYN VAUGHAN-LEE.[3] He points out that, throughout history, many spiritual seekers have encountered the Divine as a Beloved. According to Sufis, the first stage of spiritual growth is *tauba*, which means change of heart or repentance. In mystical terms, this refers to an awakening of the spiritual self, the recognition of the difference between one's faults and the perfection of the Beloved. The Sufi mystic and poet Rumi is particularly well known for his approach to the Divine as Beloved, and for the breathtaking poetry that reveals his ecstatic union.

2. Jean Houston, *The Search for the Beloved: Journeys in Mythology and Sacred Psychology* (New York: Jeremy P. Tarcher/Perigee Books, 1987).

3. Llewellyn Vaughan-Lee, *The Bond with the Beloved: The Mystical Relationship of the Lover and the Beloved.* (Inverness, Calif.: The Golden Sufi Center, 1993).

CHRISTIAN MYSTICISM

There is a wealth of material written by Christian mystics regarding the suffering and joy of the mystical experience. In particular, Teresa of Avila's sixth mansion seems appropriate to the earlier phase of my "crosses" period of spiritual development, the wilderness wandering. The sixth level comes after the spiritual betrothal of the fifth, in which the visionary experienced the initial joy of union. In the sixth stage, however, Teresa describes a period of many afflictions; some are physical and some are emotional, such as depression. This depression she likens to the tortures of hell, yet she says that one must walk through all of the tortures to reach the final mansion.

Teresa, who uses a silkworm analogy to explain spiritual growth, as does Swedenborg, points out that the silkworm must die. So must the ego of the seeker approach death in order to reach union. Despite the trials of this mansion, there are also gifts of rapture in prayer. These moments can enable the seeker to feel very close to God. I suspect that my experience at my ordination was such rapture.

After the suffering and confusion of the sixth mansion, Teresa enters the seventh mansion, the place of the spiritual marriage with Christ. She writes of the Lord's appearing in the center of the soul through an intellectual vision. She claims to have had many visions of Christ of the imaginary and intellectual kind, ones in which Christ seems to communicate directly to the soul rather than through one's faculties, such as in a physical manifestation or as a disembodied voice. The Lord does sometimes speak through our physical ears or appear to the physical eyes, but this is rare and not something that

Teresa experienced. God also speaks and appears through imagery, where we hear God or see an image within our soul. What seems to be most common is our intellect's or spirit's *sensing* the presence or understanding the message. Teresa felt many of her visions and voices were in this category.[4] I believe that, when I heard a voice in my head, it was a Teresean "intellectual" hearing where my spirit understood although my physical ears heard nothing.

For Teresa, a union takes place in the core of the soul where one cannot be separated from God. Teresa says that, in the seventh mansion, Mary and Martha become one, so that the mystic becomes active in the world. This "unified" person loses absorption in self and becomes focused on serving God.

EVELYN UNDERHILL speaks vividly of a dark night of the soul as being an intensely stagnant period, which comes between the first part of the mystical journey and union. There are rarely psychic experiences here, few ecstatic interludes to lighten the burden.[5]

However, according to Underhill, when one reaches the final mystical stage, union, there are two primary paths. For some, the self becomes transmuted into the Divine. For others, the soul enters into intimate relationship with the Divine in a spiritual marriage

---

4. Teresa of Avila, *The Interior Castle*, trans. Kieran Kavanaugh and Otillio Rodriguez (New York: Paulist Press, 1979), 178–184. For further discussion on this, see *The Book of Her Life*, Chapter 28.
5. Evelyn Underhill, *Mysticism: The Preeminent Study in the Nature and Development of Spiritual Consciousness* (New York: Doubleday, 1990), 381.

The mystic for whom intimate and personal communion has been the mode under which he best apprehended Reality speaks of the consummation of this communion, its perfect and permanent form, as the *Spiritual Marriage* of his soul with God.[6]

Thus, the dark night of wilderness wandering eventually give way to the mystical marriage. The Christian tradition is rich in its approach to God as a Beloved. I discovered soul mates back in the twelfth century, during the time of the troubadours, the courtly poets and musicians who wandered the countryside and dedicated their songs to a particular lady. Usually, she was married, but the lover worshiped her at a respectful distance, sort of as a religious man might worship the Virgin Mary—or, at least, that was the literary convention. Some of the troubadours, however, even joined monasteries.

This was the period of the "love mystics" or "bridal mysticism." One of the earliest of these mystics was BERNARD OF CLAIRVAUX who died in 1153. Bernard, like so many others, was greatly inspired by the *Song of Songs*. He saw it as depicting the relationship between the soul and the Divine. He also wrote about this relationship as being a marriage between the Bride (the soul) and the Bridegroom (Christ). This is where the term "bridal mysticism" comes from.

Another book was enormously helpful: *Hadewijch and Her Sisters: Other Ways of Loving and Knowing.*[7] Its main focus is that a thirteenth-century woman,

---

6. Ibid., 415.
7. John Giles Milhaven, *Hadewijch and Her Sisters: Other Ways of Loving and Knowing* (New York: State University of New York Press, 1993).

107

HADEWIJCH, had a mutual, *embodied* relationship with the Divine.

A number of women of this time wanted to make religious vows of some sort, but didn't want to join the convents and take vows to the church. So these women—many of them from noble families—lived in community together, observing vows of poverty, service, and celibacy as long as they were in the community. Unlike formal religious, they could leave at any time. They were called "Beguines."

Hadewijch was a Beguine and mystic in the Low Countries. She wrote hundreds of pages of her experiences, which were read and circulated for years after her death. She influenced many other mystics after her, especially John of Ruusbroec. Yet, by the 1500s, nothing more was heard about her works until they were rediscovered in 1838. Historians of mystical traditions have largely ignored her until recently. But Hadewijch was someone who had a profound mystical union with Christ.

For her, the ultimate goal in life is union with Christ. What makes Hadewijch unique, however, is that she claims her relationship with God is a mutual one—that she satisfies him and meets needs in him as well as God's satisfying her. This gives God a kind of human dimension that is not always present in mysticism.

One modern Christian mystic who writes about the traditional stages of mysticism is BERNADETTE ROBERTS.[8]

---

8. Bernadette Roberts, *The Path to No Self: Life at the Center* (Albany, N.Y.: State University of New York Press, 1991); and *The Experience of No-Self: A Contemplative Journey* (Albany, N.Y.: State University of New York Press, 1993).

She says that, in her own experience, the unitive state is an irreversible, egoless state that eventually makes "no-self" possible. For Roberts, years of testing and transformation of the self follow once spiritual marriage is achieved. It is not a state of perpetual bliss.

I think that EMANUEL SWEDENBORG himself had a dark night of the soul, as attested in his dream diary. Almost immediately after his ecstatic experience of encountering Jesus Christ in April 1744, hard lessons began. He recounts in the *Journal of Dreams*, entry 61, that he must come to understand humility and come to terms with his sinfulness:

> I have now learned this in spiritual [things], that there is nothing for it but to humble oneself and to desire nothing else, and this with all humility, than the grace of Christ. . . . I was obliged with humblest prayers to beg for forgiveness before my conscience could be pacified; for I was still in temptation until this was done.

Wilson Van Dusen, the commentator on Swedenborg's dream journal, points out that Swedenborg then had a series of dreams in which the number "two" played a significant part:

> What [Swedenborg] had been given was the number two, the relationship of God and man. He later called this "conjunction." He goes through some further temptation in which his old natural way of thinking seems opposed to the spirit. . . . He is experiencing the old Swedenborg, who is full of thoughts . . . and the new Swedenborg, who wants just to be in accord with the Spirit of God. . . . Another way of saying this

109

is that a new Swedenborg is forming, but the old one can still butt in."[9]

In his journal, Swedenborg described this period as one of temptation. He wrote that he sometimes broke out in hot sweats and frequently burst into tears at joy over God's grace. Van Dusen says, "In a way he is being ground down to a very ordinary, humble man."[10]

Swedenborg's dreams continued to reflect themes of sin and melancholy. Van Dusen concludes that this melancholy is a spiritual one, rooted in a longing for God. It is not a typical depression, although it has some of the same symptoms. These feelings seem similar to the ones I had wandering through the wilderness.

Swedenborg also had to confront many of his basic issues, as I did. He contended in particular with pride, recording this in dream entry 85:

> Afterwards I saw all that was unclean, and recognized myself as unclean, unclean with filth from head to foot. Cried, "Mercy of Jesus Christ."

Indeed, a number of subsequent dreams record his turmoil. Van Dusen refers to these experiences as being "like hell" and being an experience of the "dark side of the spiritual."[11] Yet, Swedenborg seemed to make

---

9. *Journal of Dreams*, 54. Van Dusen also suggests that many of us have had periods when we try to think spiritual thoughts, but keep getting pulled back to earthly matters. Such an experience can be annoying, but is part of rapid growth and is something that many mystics have gone through.

10. Ibid., 56.

11. Ibid., 70

progress at letting go of old issues while being prepared for his future work.

Eventually it became clear that, when he thought about God, Swedenborg felt within divine grace. Otherwise, he felt tremendous torment. He was moving toward the point when he would give up his work on his scientific studies and turn to theological writing. In commenting on Swedenborg's journal, Van Dusen says:

> Above all, I'd like the reader to get the impression of the usefulness of the dark negative side. It is not just something bad to be removed, for it serves the good. It is as intelligently designed as the heavenly side; it is useful; it aids the illumination of the good by contrast, as dark delineates the light. This, of course, also corresponds to the heaven and hell of theology, for these are the ultimates of the same process that turns up naturally in our lowly lives and dreams.[12]

Thus, after his incredible encounter with Christ on April 6, 1744, Swedenborg went through months of struggles, mood swings, and bouts of depression. When I learned this, I felt less alone in my wilderness years that followed my ecstatic Christ experiences.

In other of his works, Swedenborg speaks about a period of despair that must precede regeneration, a time he called "vastation":

> They who are being reformed are reduced into ignorance of truth, or desolation, even to grief and despair, and they then for the first time have comfort and help from the Lord. . . . What is good,

---

12. Ibid., 166.

> nay, what is blessed and happy, no one can per-
> ceive with an exquisite sense unless he has been
> in a state of what is not good, not blessed, and not
> happy.
>
> *Arcana Coelestia*, 2694: 2

This period of despair can occur either on earth or
later in the afterlife. Swedenborg sees it as a kind of
wilderness experience. Indeed, in *Arcana Coelestia*
2708:6, he states that "the journeyings and wanderings
of the people of Israel in the wilderness represented
nothing but the vastation and desolation of believers
before reformation."

Swedenborg says that one must go through vastation in order to reach what he calls redemption:

> They who are of the church are reduced to a state
> of ignorance, and also of temptation, in order that
> the evils and falsities with them may be separated
> and as it were dispersed. They who emerge from
> this kind of vastation are they who are specifically
> called the redeemed, for they are then instructed
> in the goods and truths of faith, and are reformed
> and regenerated by the Lord.
>
> *Arcana Coelestia* 2959:1

In his *Spiritual Diary* 5071, he notes that these periods can last for a very long time.

> Vastations last, with some, a long time, according
> to the quantity and quality of the good or evil.
> They are wont to continue for several years; and
> when persons are vastated, they are vastated from
> the head even to the heel; for thus has the good,
> or evil, transcribed itself upon the body.

Swedenborg suggests that vastation occurs both prior to reformation and during reformation. For me, I think of my dark night of the soul as part of the reformation process. I suspect that all of these stages occur in varying order in all of us, and, in fact, are usually more of a spiral than a ladder.

Of course, Swedenborg emerged from his own dark night and entered union. It seems that he experienced union with the Lord a year after his initial Christ vision. He had been through the experiences related in the *Journal of Dreams*, which seemed to allude to a wilderness wandering. Late in his life, he related to an acquaintance, Carl Robsahm, that, early in 1745, he was enjoying a midday meal at an inn when it grew dark; the floor seemed covered with snakes and frogs and crawling creatures. Once the darkness lifted, he saw a figure in the corner telling him not to eat so much. Then there was blackness and then a clearing, and he was alone in the room. Robsahm states in his memoirs of the Swedish seer that Swedenborg then said:

> I went home; and during the night the same man revealed himself to me again, but I was not frightened now. He then said that He was the Lord God, the Creator of the world, and the Redeemer, and that He had chosen me to explain to men the spiritual sense of the Scripture, and that He Himself would explain to me what I should write on this subject; that same night also were opened to me, so that I became thoroughly convinced of their reality, the worlds of spirits, heaven and hell, and I recognized there many acquaintances of every condition in life. From that day I gave up the study of all worldly science, and laboured in

113

spiritual things, according as the Lord had commanded me to write.[13]

Cyriel Sigstedt, one of Swedenborg's biographers, says of this experience that "the first phase of his life now was ended. . . . By the remarkable vision of April 1745, the meaning of his life had been explained to him and his sadness had been turned into joy, his disquietude into comforting assurance. A commission had been given him by the Lord. . . . Swedenborg entered upon an exhaustive study of the Sacred Scriptures."[14]

Swedenborg's empathy with those who embark on a spiritual journey can be found everywhere in his writings. One of the most important tenets of Swedenborgian theology is the concept of the "Divine–Human." To Swedenborg, the passion on the cross is not the key to salvation. The key is all of the human actions the Lord performed through his life that allowed the Divine to come closer, until they became one, finally, on the cross. In *True Christian Religion* 97, Swedenborg refers to this process of union as glorification, a sort of heavenly marriage. We humans can go through the process of regeneration, in which we act in charity, the Lord comes closer to us, and we enter into union. He mentions this joining also in *Arcana Coelestia* 10067:7:

> The Lord regenerates man as he glorified his Human. . . . This conjunction is reciprocally

13. "Robsahm's Memoirs of Swedenborg," in R. L. Tafel, ed., *Documents concerning the Life and Character of Emanuel Swedenborg* (London: Swedenborg Society, 1875), I, 36.

14. Cyriel Sigstedt, *The Swedenborg Epic: The Life and Works of Emanuel Swedenborg* (London: Swedenborg Society, 1981), 203.

accomplished by means of good, and is called the
heavenly marriage, and is heaven with man.

Swedenborg is clear, however, that it is not the human
who joins with the Lord. Rather, out of free will, the
human being chooses to avoid engaging in evil and the
Lord unites with the human. It is, therefore, not by our
faith that we enter into union with the Divine, but
rather by the good with which we live our lives.

All of this helps me understand my years of withdrawal from God. Swedenborg says joining with the
Lord needs to be reciprocal and that, if we don't partici-
pate in it, "conjunction is not effected, but withdrawal
and a consequent separation, yet not on the Lord's part,
but on man's part." In order to become part of that conjunction, we are given the choice of walking toward
heaven or toward hell, he tells us in *True Christian Religion* 371:2.

In reading Swedenborg, I understood why I was so
drawn to the human Jesus. Swedenborg writes that our
union is not with "his Supreme Divine Itself" but with
"his Divine Human," for it is through the human part of
the Divine where we can feel most readily connected.
Swedenborg was very clear about the importance of regeneration's being external as well as internal. Again, it
all comes back to how we live our lives, how we relate to
others on this earth, not just to our relationship with
God and not to the mystical experiences we may have.

Swedenborg wrote a great deal about the concept of
union, a concept that gets to the heart of his theology on
redemption. Again, the reason Jesus came into the world,
according to Swedenborg, is that the Divine could not
reach the human race any longer, so the Lord came into
the world. Through the experiences of temptations and

finally death on the cross, the Human and the Divine were united into one.

> The passion of the cross was the extremity of the Lord's temptation, by which he fully united his human to his Divine and his Divine to his human, and thus glorified himself. This very union is the means by which those who have the faith in him, which is the faith of charity, can be saved.
>
> *Arcana Coelestia 2776:2*

A similar experience is available to humans, but with a different name. In *Arcana Coelestia* 2004:3, Swedenborg writes that "between the Lord and Jehovah there was complete oneness, but between man and the Lord there is union." Another difference is that the Lord united himself to Jehovah by his own power, but humanity does not have this power, so "the Lord joins man with Himself." It is through love and charity that a human becomes one with the Lord. "This 'being one' is that mystical union which some think about, and which is by love alone" (*Arcana Coelestia* 1013:3).

This oneness exists on a larger scale than human/divine, as Swedenborg goes on to explain in the next paragraph:

> Each society, which consists of many, constitutes as if it were one man. And all the societies together—or the universal heaven—constitute one man, which is also called the Grand Man. . . . The universal heaven is a likeness of the Lord, for the Lord is the all in all who are therein.

This remarkable form—in which the least is a precise reflection of the greatest—shows that the union of the Son and the Father was meant also to indicate the unity of the Lord and humanity, which is the very purpose of the Lord's coming into the world. Through his taking on human nature, there resulted an inflow of the Divine with the human.

It seems that, in some ways, our task is simply to recognize this inflow that is always occurring. In other respects, we need to engage in the process of regeneration. Just as the Lord experienced glorification in achieving union with Jehovah, we must engage in regeneration in order to achieve oneness with the Lord.

Swedenborg's approach gives me a clearer understanding of what I was going through. I was walking through the process of regeneration and, in doing so, had come to recognize that the Lord and I were in union. Just as Jesus had to come to terms with the divine and human dimensions of himself, I had to come to terms with my human essence and its divine influx. It sounds simple enough as Swedenborg writes about it, but I knew from my experiences that it was the agonizing process of my ego's encountering the Lord.

QUESTIONS FOR
JOURNALING AND DISCUSSION

1. Have you had times of wilderness wanderings, where you felt distant from God and confused about your spiritual life? Reflect on these periods as a necessary stage in spiritual life. Where was God during these times?

2. Consider this statement from Swedenborg: "The journeyings and wanderings of the people of Israel in the wilderness represented . . . the vastation and desolation . . . before reformation." Look at your periods of spiritual crisis and see what emerges for you.

3. Have you had times when you felt certain of God's presence with you or of an inner assurance in your mind? Even though you may not have "heard" or "seen" God with your physical ears and eyes, could any of these times have been what Teresa describes as visions of image or intellect? Reflect on these times, and what it was that lead you to believe that God was with you.

4. Swedenborg talks of God's being pro-active in entering our lives. In what ways do you think that the Lord is attempting to come closer in your life?

5. How do you respond to efforts of the Lord to move closer toward you or into union? Are there issues from your other relationships in life that you take to the divine relationship? What are some of those issues, and how do they block you from reaching union with the Divine?

6. Do you have spiritual disciplines in your life that you are able to perform most days? Are there some you would like to add?

PART 3

CHAKRAS
1995–PRESENT

Kundalini

It was a cold Saturday evening in January 1995, and I had a roaring fire in my woodstove. On this evening, I put my yoga mat in front of the fire and began my routine of yoga postures.

As I moved into the postures, I felt a sudden rush of energy at the base of my spine. I intuitively trusted that this energy issued from the Lord and surrendered myself fully to its experience. At that moment, I felt the energy "whooshing" up my spine to the top of my head. I collapsed on the mat, in a state of ecstasy. I felt the oneness with the Divine. No longer was there an "I" and "Thou," but only a grand oneness of all things together. I lay on the mat savoring the connectedness and glad to have the bliss in place of an "I" identity. All along my spine, I felt alive and energized. It seemed that every part of me was in balance. No longer was I struggling to

121

understand my relationship with the Divine; there was no need of relationship. Only being.

I wondered if I had encountered the kundalini energy.

I delved into materials on the kundalini and learned that concepts of the kundalini come originally from the Hindu tradition, from the ancient sacred writings, the Vedas. They present the system of yoga, which means union, particularly union between one's ego-self and one's deepest spiritual self. However, concepts of the kundalini have appeared in most of the religious traditions, including the Jewish *davven* (a rocking of the upper body during prayer), the Pentecostal charismatics, the Quakers, the Shakers, and with African dance.

Psychologist Bonnie Greenwell says that her research has convinced her that, when people meditate or pray, they can become open to the ancient Indian concept of *Sat-chit-ananda. Sat* is the essence in all things. *Chit* is universal knowledge. *Ananda* is ecstasy. The experience of this level of consciousness is one that can awaken energies known as kundalini.[1]

Greenwell sees the kundalini as an experience that is described in many traditions. Among the Christian mystics who have encountered such phenomena, she lists Hildegard of Bingen, Meister Eckhard, St. Catherine of Genoa, St. Catherine of Siena, St. John of the Cross, St. Paul, St. Teresa of Avila, Teilhard de Chardin, Jacob Boehme, and Emanuel Swedenborg.

Once awakened, these energies can begin a process of spiritual growth that lasts for years. Following

---

1. Bonnie Greenwell, *Energies of Transformation: A Guide to the Kundalini Process* (Saratoga, Calif.: Shakti River Press, 1995), 2.

the initial awakening, one can encounter psychic phenomena, extrasensory perceptions, and a range of emotional upheavals.[2]

I discovered that many writers on the subject see a connection between the awakening of kundalini and activation of the body's energy centers or chakras. These researchers believe that, as the kundalini rises in a person, it activates each center, and particular types of life lessons are triggered and come into consciousness. In addition to Greenwell, authors Carolyn Myss, Harish Johari, and Rosalyn Bruyere also take this approach. Bruyere says that the concept of chakras was in the Greek mystery schools and later a part of early Christian mysticism. Around the turn of the century, the concept came back into Western mysticism through the theosophists who traveled to India. Myss sees the seven sacraments of the Roman Catholic Church as serving a similar symbolic function as the chakras in representing stages of spiritual growth. Sannella discusses the kundalini in a number of cultural traditions, including the Christian.

Lotuses often depict the chakras because, with the eyes closed, there is often a visual experience of endless billowing, which looks like the unfolding of the petals of the flower. As the kundalini reaches a chakra, that lotus is said to open its flower. As the kundalini leaves a particular chakra, its petals close and hang down to

---

2. Ibid., 2–3. See also Lee Sannella, *The Kundalini Experience: Psychosis or Transcendence?* (Lower Lake, Calif.: Integral Publishing, 1992) for an account of various physical, emotional, and spiritual phenomena related to the kundalini.

demonstrate that the particular chakra's energies are now activated and open to the kundalini.[3]

Some chakra specialists might say that the experiences I was having in my yoga practice were encounters with *pranotthana* energy, which were opening my energy centers and presenting me with unresolved life issues.

The first chakra lessons are often said to be around one's relationship with community and symbolizing the earth and its lessons involved in letting go of insecurity about physical survival. The second chakra, or water chakra, is often seen as teaching about the emotions, personal power, lineage survival, and sexual passion.[4]

Issues of family, relationship, and physical health remained significant issues for me during the next two years. As I confronted these issues, I also tried to learn more about the kundalini and chakras. An opportunity presented itself in the fall of 1995.

I had to make a trip to San Francisco. The Swedenborg School of Religion had asked me to attend a conference on working with conflict issues in Asian–American congregations.

I accepted eagerly. But only part of my motivation was to attend the workshop. The other was to see if I could contact an expert in kundalini energy: Dr. Stuart Sovatsky, a psychologist at the San Francisco Kundalini

3. Ajit Mookerjee, *Kundalini: The Arousal of the Inner Energy* (Rochester, Vt.: Destiny Books, 1986), 39. The exact number of chakras differs with various traditions and writers.

4. David Frawley, *Tantric Yoga and the Wisdom Goddesses: Spiritual Secrets of Ayurveda* (Salt Lake City, Utah: Passage Press, 1994), 174–176; and personal correspondence with Stuart Sovatsky, 1999. See also Myss and Greenwell on this topic for more perspectives on what the various chakras represent.

Clinic, whose work I had encountered in my reading. I made an appointment to see him at his home office.

I summarized for him the spiritual journey I had been on, from my early days of spiritual awakening through my wilderness wanderings and encounters with Christ. I talked about my sense of entering a mystical marriage at the convention of 1994. I explained that now I was doing yoga and meditation and was experiencing powerful energies moving up my spine.

"I've been feeling intense energies pouring into my root chakra, then feeling it shoot up my spine. And as it makes its way up my spine, I go through intense connectedness with Christ. It's a total surrender of my ego to this divine love; then the energy reaches the crown chakra and every part of me seems totally merged into oneness with the Divine. It's the union experience all over again. It has happened from time to time these past months, and always I feel it comes from grace. Does this sound like experience with the kundalini?"

Dr. Sovatsky assured me that my experience sounded like the kundalini, or more precisely, pranotthana energy, which precedes the full kundalini awakening. He explained that medieval mystics who experienced the feeling of Christ so intensely were probably also experiencing pranotthana and kundalini transformations of energy, but they wrote of their experiences in a kind of code. Only those who had had similar experiences could crack the code and feel a fellowship with other mystics.

One of the most important things Dr. Sovatsky told me was that, by further working with yoga and postures, I could develop the ability to activate the kundalini, so that the experience could be controlled. He felt that this was important because it seemed as if my

125

own experience was a matter of grace rather than concentrated effort. He also indicated that learning more about the role of chakras in the process would be beneficial. Yogis throughout history have learned a great deal about the body. The physical body is only one aspect of our being; there are also subtle bodies around it and chakras along the spine that regulate the energy.

With this knowledge and the incentive of learning more about the kundalini experience, I left Dr. Sovatsky's office to visit Grace Cathedral with its wonderful labyrinth. The labyrinth is a walking meditation based on an ancient design that is considered sacred, a replica of one at Chartres, France, where medieval pilgrims used to make yearly journeys in lieu of visits to the Holy Land. There was a large labyrinth design on the carpet at the rear of the nave, but folding chairs had been set up over it for a concert. I was disappointed because I obviously could not walk on a labyrinth that was obscured. But I soon found out that there was a stone terrazzo labyrinth in the beautiful, large plaza overlooking a park and, in the distance, the bay.

I stared at it for a few minutes. It looked very simple; surely it wouldn't take more than a couple of minutes to get to the center and then to walk back out again. I took a deep breath and began the path into the maze. Quickly, I realized it was far more complex than it had appeared. I walked and walked and walked, at times getting close to the center but then finding the path leading me away. Twice, I ended up back at the beginning without ever having made it to the center.

I was frustrated. "I'm so stupid, I can't even walk this silly path that people have walked for centuries!"

I decided to give it one more try. This time as I began, I felt the Lord's presence. I realized I had ignored prayer the first two times into the labyrinth and had felt that I was walking alone. This time, I knew the Lord was with me, and I tried to focus on our relationship and not get distracted by the shimmering bay in the distance. How like the spiritual journey, I thought. It's so important to stay focused and keep asking for help so as not to get sidetracked.

Again, I walked and walked, sometimes thinking I was almost at the center only to find the path meandering towards the outer edges of the labyrinth. As I walked, I prayed.

"This is a hard path, Lord. You push me into my feelings and keep confronting me with myself. You never let me escape from who I am, from what our relationship is all about. Sometimes I get tired of working so hard. You know it's not easy being in relationship with you. It's no bed of roses. It's incredibly hard work, day by day, step by step."

I kept walking and walking. Only later did I read that the path is one-third of a mile to the center. As I walked, all frustration seemed to dissipate. I began feeling more at peace.

All of a sudden, I found myself at the center. A silly little thing, really, to have walked to the center of some markings in stone, but it had taken me nearly an hour of effort to get there. It felt like a stupendous accomplishment. I closed my eyes, feeling the warmth of the sun and the gentle breeze from the bay, feeling connected with the Lord. I loved feeling united, knowing I was part of a much larger wholeness. I felt the Lord's presence in my life and in the world. There was no more anger for what God didn't do in my life, only gratitude for what God was doing and a realization of how much work I

127

needed to do to make change happen. I felt humble, grateful, and loved by my Beloved. I was balanced again.

I realized I had been struggling with surrendering my will to the Lord. But I was starting to see it not as a struggle between myself and another being, but rather a struggle *within me*. When I experienced kundalini energy, it seemed so clear that there was no struggle. There was nothing to be surrendered. There was only Being.

The walk back through the labyrinth was easy and made with a light heart. I made it in no time, eager to get back to my life, back to understanding how the spiritual can lead me to fight social oppression. But first I had a few more hours in San Francisco, so I walked in the direction of Chinatown, eager to enjoy my final hours as a tourist before the work must begin again.

My spiritual life was shaken deeply only a few month's later. I faced my father's death on Christmas Day, 1995. Dad hadn't been well in a long time; and my brother, sister-in-law, and I all suspected this would be our last Christmas together. We planned a big celebration at dad's house for Christmas Eve but were shocked that, a few days before, he became very ill and was rushed to the hospital. We all got to the hospital as quickly as we could and spent our last few days with dad as he slowly slipped away.

As dad entered the spirit world that Christmas morning, I realized I no longer had a parent living on the earth. I felt the aloneness of an orphan. Knowing dad had been reunited with mom in the spiritual world did not lessen my own grief.

I faced a long winter of deep feelings that kept rising to the surface. It seemed that every loss in my life came back into consciousness, and even my spiritual practices could not erase the feelings. Actually, I

128

suspected that my spiritual work was bringing the feelings to the surface. But I also felt that the spiritual work would help me resolve the issues.

Slowly, I was learning how to control the pranot-thana energy, as Dr. Sovatsky had suggested. It rarely came by grace any more; now I had to work with postures, meditation, and breathing to access it. Then, it would move slowly, staying primarily in the first few chakras. This, I thought, was perhaps where my lessons were. Issues of security, identity in the world, relationships with others are all considered issues of the lower chakras. I felt the energy in those centers during my yoga, and I encountered those life lessons throughout my days as I struggled to integrate my father's death.

A new year came. As the winter of 1995 turned to the spring of 1996, I began to feel energy moving into my fourth chakra, which is said to be located near the heart and is the center of love. My love for my Beloved was being rekindled. I turned to books again to find others who wrote about these experiences and rediscovered *The Bond with the Beloved* by Sufi teacher Llewellyn Vaughan-Lee. I read his book over and over again, underlining my favorite passages. I was thrilled to learn that he would be giving a workshop in New York State. I signed up and spent a Memorial Day weekend with Sufis that year. I was preoccupied, however, as I had just been told that my routine mammogram screening showed some suspicious calcium deposits. I was scheduled for a biopsy after the workshop.

Coalescence

I arrived at the Phoenicia Center in the Catskills for a
retreat with Llewellyn Vaughan-Lee. I had taken my
time in making the trip because I didn't want to feel any
stress about arriving by a certain time; I thought that, if
it turned out that I did have cancer, it would be very important to avoid stress. Then I thought that, even if I
don't have cancer, being stress-free would be a good way
to live life!

I loved listening to Vaughan-Lee that night. He
talked about mysticism, stressing that the Sufis are a
path of mysticism, not just spirituality. He explained the
difference between the two: spirituality seeks for purpose
and meaning, while mysticism seeks nothing. The mystic works to annihilate the ego, to let go of attachments
and meanings. To be nothing. Just to be. Surrender is the
most important thing, and the simplest, yet is the hardest to do.

It was my good fortune to be able to speak with Vaughan-Lee during a break in the workshop. I told him how much I had loved his book *Bond with the Beloved*. I explained about my Swedenborgianism and recounted the union experience that happened at communion two years ago, my feeling of being connected with Christ. And how I fell in love and have had an intense relationship of ups and downs since. And how much I got from the Christian love mystics, including the Beguines as well as from his writings and those of other Sufis.

Vaughan-Lee stated that his book was actually based on Teresa's four stages of prayer (recollection, quiet, union, and ecstasy) and that he used many Christian mystics in writing it. He examines a universal mystical experience, not one limited to a specific tradition.

He explained that Sufism is a path of love in which God is experienced as the Beloved. Although there are many different forms of Sufism, Sufis are essentially lovers of God. There were only a small number of love mystics in Christian history, and many of them were persecuted. With the Sufi tradition, I felt a fellowship not unlike the feeling I have when reflecting on the Swedenborgian mystical tradition. The Sufis aim to achieve oneness with the Beloved; this process is part of the Sufi mystical path.

Despite feeling at home with the Sufis, I know that I am deeply rooted in the Christian tradition. The experience of the Christian mystics seem to form my home base, a home that I always return to even though I want and need to explore other parts of the mystical world. Still, there is a wonderful affirmation in finding kinship and knowing that people throughout the ages and from every country on earth and in every culture have shared the mystical experience.

But it wasn't only an affinity with the Sufis that I experienced at this workshop. I also experimented with visualization. I concentrated on my breast, feeling the hand of God pulling out malignancy, transforming it, and releasing it into the universe. I felt my anger at the possible invasion of a foreign substance and called on God to remove any disease, although it seemed appropriate to use affirmation, visualizations, and other healing techniques to facilitate my own healing. I knew, however, that I would accept God's will.

Much of what Vaughan-Lee said supported those various reactions. He talked of letting go of all attachments, even the attachment to the spiritual experience. Sufis, he stated, live in the world as their place of purification, although everything is offered back to God.

During the afternoon meditation, I felt the oneness and the ecstasy. It seemed so clear to me that life and death are one, that, on the mystical level, it makes no difference whether I have cancer or not, whether I live or die. All is oneness in God, despite the external circumstances. This feels like enlightenment. This is the basic truth all mystics— including Swedenborg—have identified: a oneness beyond duality.

I realize that my own mystical journey is one where mysticism took me by surprise and I resisted it. Then I accepted it and even learned how to open myself to the ecstasy through meditation, prayer, yoga, and chakra work. But I must learn to stay active in the world. I see activity as a form of mysticism. At times, suffering and pain are part of life in the world, but the ecstasy always comes back eventually. It's important to experience whatever life offers and to be grateful for it as a gift. Even if I were found to have cancer (perhaps especially if I do), I need to be grateful for the gift of learning and serving.

Soon after my weekend with the Sufis, it was time for my biopsy. I found that I was able to face it with a fair amount of calm. I knew I wasn't afraid of death, but I was nervous about encountering pain. I used my meditations and my breathing to deal with the pain and discomforts that would be presented that day.

I got through the biopsy without distress. I stayed the night before with Sisters of Mercy near the hospital. That morning I got up early to pray, meditate, and do yoga before leaving for the hospital. One of the Sisters dropped me off, and I arrived feeling relaxed at 6:30 in the morning. I didn't have surgery until 10:00, so I managed to spend most of that time meditating. I stayed completely relaxed as the IV was put into my arm.

Actually, my surgical experience was not all that traumatic. I was told that I had awakened during the surgery and told everyone that I had a dream about being in a garden and seeing flowers. The nurses were impressed that I felt so good so quickly. I did not experience much pain from the incision. During the evening, if I felt an ache, I used my hand to send energy that released the pain. I never did use the pain medication that was prescribed.

I was and continue to be grateful for all that I learned about meditation and surrender and positive thinking. I ended up feeling I could handle any further treatments. I wrote in my journal, "I so hope it's benign, but then I trust God to make this decision. I really trust in the outcome and feel a lot of peace about it."

My one sadness was that I was told to wait a week before resuming yoga again. Although my breast was

133

sore and the incision had to heal, my body missed my postures.

Within a few days, I had the results, and they were somewhat confusing. I have "lobular carcinoma in situ," which means that there are cancerous cells in my lobes, but not in the ducts. As I understand it, the cells in the lobes won't cause me any problems. But they could move to Stage I cancer. I am at high risk for breast cancer, but my best chance of avoiding it, the doctor said, is to focus on a low-stress lifestyle and a healthy diet.

I felt calm knowing all of this. It seemed to be time to take a hard look at my life and determine which activities I felt most called to do and which ones could be cut out. It also seemed a good time to consider making some significant changes in my lifestyle.

My lifestyle and my body became the focus of my prayer and meditation for weeks. It occurred to me that perhaps I was working on fifth chakra issues, which are often seen as purification and communication. I read everything I could find on cancer-free lifestyle changes. I decided on a largely macrobiotic diet, since I preferred vegetarian eating anyway, and a diet heavy in soy products is thought by some to enhance protection from breast cancer. Exercise, meditation, and yoga would need to continue being an important dimension of my daily life. Still, I felt that the focus of my daily practices needed to be prayer and scripture-reading, with regular supplemental reading from my spiritual mentor, Swedenborg. My commitment to staying close in my relationship with the Lord had to be the heart of my spiritual work. It seemed closely related to my heart-centered chakra work. I was understanding what things were nearest to my heart.

Yet, the further my spiritual path unfolded, the less

important my spiritual disciplines seemed to be and the more important my daily life became. What did it matter what I read or experienced if I couldn't take it into my life?

I was feeling closer than ever to Swedenborg's philosophy, which emphasizes not the mystical experience, but rather how one lives one's life. He supported and affirmed mystical experience, but never elevated it. The person who lived a good life without mystical experience was far more spiritual than the person who had many mystical experiences, but could never take them into daily living.

Deciding how to use my time as a way of living my spirituality seemed particularly important now that I was facing the finite nature of earthly life. I could develop cancer at any point, and it could take me to my death. Or I could live a long time on this earthly plane. Either way, every day and every moment took on great significance. Life was a precious gift not to be wasted.

In making these decisions, I realized that the questions had changed for me. No longer could I ask: What do I most want to do? What would make me happiest? What path would give me the most serene life? The question had become: what do I believe the Lord wants me to do?

I was coming to realize what a dramatic shift in perspective that change was. Understanding one's call (and I don't mean just to "ordained" ministry, but the life calls we all have) involves setting aside the ego. My ego-self seemed to want comforts, happiness, financial success, easy work, affirmation, and so forth. The Lord, I felt, wanted me to fulfill missions of service that might be difficult, might not be financially rewarding, and would not necessarily result in appreciation or acclaim from others.

135

When I started to doubt that God's calls are like this, I remembered the life of Jesus. Our rewards come from the joy of union with the Lord and service to others, rather than from earthly pleasures and affirmations.

So what did it seem that God was calling me to do with the rest of my life? I continued to feel a strong call to ordained ministry in the Swedenborgian Church, and, at least for that time, to my job at the Swedenborg School of Religion.

I also felt drawn toward staying involved with a vital source of spiritual and political energy in New Hampshire, the Sisters of Mercy. Being a part of their justice team gave me an opportunity to work with other spiritually committed women at defining the most important state issues in which to have an impact. The Mercies are particularly devoted to women and children.

Although I decided to let my regular social-work practice dwindle, I wanted to continue being involved with the activities of social workers in the state. I was on a committee working with legislative issues and on one involving support for political candidates in our state elections. Staying on both these committees for the present also felt important, since the state political arena was one place where I wanted to try to make a small contribution. I remembered that Swedenborg had always considered the issues of the Swedish parliament of great importance, and he had been involved there throughout his adult life.

Unfortunately, making choices also meant that I would have to let go of some other activities. I felt that the time had come to end my work as a minister with the Network Center in Concord, New Hampshire, which I had helped establish as part of my ordained ministry with the church. It was time to leave and to allow the group to call another minister if they so chose.[1] In letting go of my regular Sunday morning commitment, I hoped that on some Sundays I could be available to parishes without ministers in the New England area.

This way of approaching life was impacting my everyday existence. I was beginning each day with prayer, asking to be used by the Lord during that day for whatever God deemed most important.

My prayers were being answered in unexpected ways. For example, in my own mind, I would have my day at the school planned. But during the hour I had set aside to do class preparations, a student with a problem might pop into my office. Being present for that situation seemed the way God wanted me to spend the hour.

At the same time, I found my work becoming more focused on detail. Attending to the minutiae of work had never been my strength. I have always been more people-oriented than paperwork-oriented. But my spiritual work was actually taking me deeper into my need to organize better. After morning prayer and meditation, I would feel myself far more able to organize my day. I found myself with renewed zest to develop a better filing system, to keep a calendar, and to manage a realistic to-do list every day. My mystical self was leading me not away from the world, but into its most minute, earthly details of daily living.

It occurred to me that perhaps I was working with sixth-chakra issues, which involve self-evaluation and reflection. Many see the sixth chakra as relating to psychic phenomena, and it appeared that I was developing a

---

1. The Network Center joined the Maine association in July 1997 and called the Reverend Nadine Cotton as its full-time minister. It is now called The Spiritual Network Center.

deeper understanding of that dimension of life. I was finding that psychic phenomena were actually less present in my life than they had been earlier in my journey. Swedenborg was one of the few seekers who could explore the world of the psychic and attend to his spiritual growth at the same time. For many of us, the psychic is a stage to be passed through, a trap to be avoided.

I noticed that, as the incidents of psychic phenomena had become fewer, the periods of bliss and ecstasy were also less frequent. My yoga work was leaving me with more of a deep serenity that lasted for hours rather than a sudden zap of bliss that disappeared in moments.

I was experiencing a new stage in my relationship with the Lord. Rather than seesawing between feelings of deep love and then distance and anger, it seemed that I had entered into a real partnership with the Lord, where we worked together.

Concerning this period of my life, I wrote in my journal,

> I'm aware of being so different inside. Something has changed. I wrote recently that I felt I had moved to another stage in my spiritual growth. In this one, I am more confident, but the "I" is less. I used to feel and often say to God, "I can't do what you're asking me to do. I'm just not capable." Now, I don't question what God asks me to do. I just assume if God asks, then I/we can do it. It's much more "we" than "I" now. It's God in me. God through me. God with me. Whatever. I am an instrument of God, rather than an "I" alone in the world.
>
> I worked hard this past week preparing the curriculum for the lay leadership training that I'll do in Urbana later this month with my colleague

Ted. I also wrote a sermon for the upcoming service I'm doing at Portland as well as a lecture for
our camp in Fryeburg, Maine. But, unlike the past,
I'm not questioning whether I can get all of those
things done on time. I just got up at 6 a.m., packed
the car with my camping gear, got up to Portland
by 10 for the service, then afterwards found the
camp and set up my tent. I feel so much less stress
than in the past. Now I feel joy in the doing of all
the tasks of my life, instead of worrying about
whether I'll get them done.

My joy runs deep. I feel deep contentment in
being a minister. It is not a job or role; it has become who I am in the world.

I feel joy in being part of a church community
as well as all of the other communities of my life.
Surely life was meant to be lived in community!

As the weeks progressed late in the fall of 1997, I
continued to feel that the "I" of my existence was becoming weaker.

For example, at one time during this period, I par-
ticipated in a workshop and had taken part in a humor-
ous role-play. At its end, I engaged in a typical train of
thought: "How did I do? What do the others think of my
performance? Were people amused? Did I offend anyone?" Then, I felt the Lord's love within me. Suddenly,
all of my internal dialogue halted. There was nothing inside but the love of the Lord. In that instant, it was clear
that all of my questions had come from my ego; I was
wondering how others perceived me when all that mattered was whether I was serving the Lord.

Soon after, I received word of the death of my
cousin. I walked through the funeral feeling that I was
living in two worlds at once. I felt sadness and grief,
but also connected with God and could see that, from

139

the Lord's perspective, nothing is really a tragedy. God is everywhere and in everything. The external "I" can encounter tragedy and feel its pain, but there is serenity deep within my soul that cannot be touched.

But, as you probably suspect by now, the spiritual journey is a never-ending one. You might reach a plateau and stay there for weeks, months, even years; but the journey must continue. Changes will take place.

Thus, I found that, just as my internal, self-critical dialogue had stopped a few weeks earlier, my ongoing dialogue with my Beloved was now also gone. There seemed to be no mystical marriage anymore. There was no inner voice, no sense of guidance. But there was peace. A profound sense of being. There was such a deep peace that I could not find fear or anxiety. More puzzling, I realized that I had been relating to the Divine through a mystical marriage, as though there were an "I" and a "he." Now, there was just being. It didn't feel as if God were gone. It was more as if a part of *me*—the part that had known God—was gone.

I realized this, oddly enough, during a specific time—during a snowstorm in November 1997, in which my car died completely on a deserted, rural road. No power in the car, no houses anywhere in sight, certainly no public telephones within walking distance: only dark night and snow quickly covering my car. I actually waited for two hours, hoping for another car to pass by. My external self was cold and hungry, yet I was completely calm and unafraid—something I would not have been had this situation occurred five years previously. I searched inside for my inner voice, for direction, yet found none. Despite this, I felt no anxiety; oddly—surprisingly, even to myself—I felt only peace. I instinctively knew that my mystical marriage had ended, yet I felt no loss, no separation. I felt that I had become a part of what I had spiritually surrendered to over the past two years.

Now, this spiritual surrender did not involve loss of consciousness, common sense, or the sense of self-preservation. After seeing that no earthly help was likely to stop for me, I walked across a hill until I spotted a house. I felt like the sole survivor of a plane crash. At any rate, the important point is not the specifics of that rather long, lonely, and potentially dangerous night, but the realization that I was entering another phase of my mystical journey.

A few months later, on Ash Wednesday, 1998, I wrote the following in my journal:

> Another Ash Wednesday, and much is very different. I'm "beyond" the mystical marriage and feeling sad and lonely for it. Yet it, too, was simply another stage in the journey. It was designed for the weaker human ego to be close to the stronger divine until the weaker was crushed and barely existed. The purpose of the mystical marriage was not to last forever, but rather for the strong to devour the weak.
>
> I don't think my ego self is gone, and it probably never will be while on the earth. But I do feel that it is weaker. I have many moments when it disappears for awhile, and there is only being. Then the ego creeps back and I take it into the world, striving to serve the divine human as best I can. That, perhaps, is what the journey is all about.

Perhaps the lessons of early 1998 were from the seventh chakra. Perhaps they were about Swedenborg's union and the divine-human relationship. It is what the

Hindus talked about with Shakti and Shiva, what the Christian mystics talked about in union with Christ.

Although we are separate, we are also one. The human, ego-filled "I" is only a part of what constitutes my identity. Because of divine influx, I am integrated with God by union. I feel more pulled than ever to be active and involved in the world. I feel the ups and downs of life. Yet, I also feel convinced of a deep pocket of serenity at the core of my soul that cannot be shaken.

I can't, of course, understand it or even put it into words. I have only a personal story that tells its version of the universal story.

This period of my journey ended as it had began.

It was the Swedenborgian Convention of 1998. Due to confusion in the schedule, it was not clear which ministers were doing which chapel services. As several of us divided up the services needing coverage, another woman minister, Gladys Wheaton, and I agreed to do the memorial communion service on Friday morning.

It seemed a special opportunity to co-celebrate as two women ministers, one African-American and one white. It was a chance to bring the convention theme of "God's Promises" into communion. We spent hours putting it together and sharing our ideas for the service.

As the service unfolded that morning, I was suffused with pure joy. I felt the joy of being with a fellow minister serving our church community. I felt the Lord with us, in us, around us. I felt the vibrant call to live passionately in the world, making spirituality real moment by moment. I felt the Divine not as parent or beloved or partner, but rather as substance—the substance of me and all of us and everything. I felt the deepest peace I had ever known. Gladys and I danced together down the aisle as we exited singing *Standing on the Promises of God* with all the participants.

I danced out the door, into the sunshine, and down the path of the rest of my life—a dance in which I am learning new steps, even as you read this book.

REFLECTIONS ON THE PAST
Chakras

T ERESA OF AVILA wrote that the person in the seventh mansion of mysticism would continue to have
trials and sufferings, yet the soul itself would be at peace.
She says it is as though there can be violence and dis-
turbances shaking the other rooms of the mansion—
they can be distressing—yet no one can force the soul to
leave its safety in its private domain. In this sanctuary,
the raptures and ecstasies of the earlier rooms occur less
frequently. The soul, however, feels peace.

Another Christian mystic who discusses this period of the mystical journey is BERNADETTE ROBERTS.
She believes that union or mystical marriage is more
commonly experienced than most realize, but many
who are in this state do not recognize it because the
available literature describes a personal experience or

revelation. In addition, much of the mystical literature implies that this state is a culmination of the spiritual journey—a goal to be achieved at the end of a process. Roberts, however, sees the unitive state as the *only* stepping stone that can lead to "no-self" or the true end of the journey. Her concepts of no-self and no-ego contrast to modern psychology, which tries to help one define the self, whereas the contemplative journey moves one to no-self.[1]

My own experience is that the mystical marriage is a stage. The peace that follows comes and goes at various levels of intensity yet contains its own set of lessons and challenges in spiritual growth. I am also not certain that earlier stages disappear forever; I suspect that we spiral in and out of many stages depending on the particular life lessons we have at a given time.

Experiencing what I consider to be kundalini energy (or more accurately, pranotthana) has been important in moving me into a feeling of "surrender" to the Lord, and then into what I call peace in being. Working with these energies through yoga and meditation has greatly intensified the speed and depth of my personal spiritual journey.

I have often wondered if EMANUEL SWEDENBORG himself experienced the kind of energy that others have called kundalini? Wilson Van Dusen thinks that he did. There are a number of times in Swedenborg's dream journal when he could be describing the kundalini energy, as, for example, in these two entries, numbers 127 and 209:

---

1. See especially chapter 2 of *The Experience of No-Self: A Contemplative Journey* and an earlier work, *The Path to No-Self: Life at the Center.* Parts of this section are based on a personal correspondence of July 26, 1999, with Roberts.

The spirit came with its heavenly life, as it were ecstatic, intense: and in a manner allowed me to go higher and higher in that state so that had I gone on higher, I should have been dissolved away by this same actual life of joy.

Something very wonderful happened to me. I came into strong shudderings, as when Christ showed me the divine grace; one followed the other, ten or fifteen in number. I waited in expectation of being thrown upon my face as the former time, but this did not occur. With the last shudder I was lifted up and with my hands I felt a back. I laid hold of the whole back, as well as put my hands under to the breast in front. Straightway it laid itself down, and I saw in front the countenance also, but this very obscurely. I was then kneeling and thought to myself whether or not I should lay myself down alongside, but this did not occur; it seemed as if it were not permitted. The shudders all started from below in the body and went up to the head.

This followed in the next entry (210):

This was in a vision when I was neither waking nor sleeping, for I had all my thoughts together. It was the inward man separated from the outward that knew this. When I was quite awake, similar shudders came over me several times. It must have been a holy angel, because I was not thrown on my face. What it could mean our Lord knows best. It seemed that it was told me in the first instance that I should have something for my guidance; or some such thing. God's grace is shown to the inward and outward man in me. To God alone be praise and honor.

Concerning entries 209 and 210, Van Dusen says:

> If you will, he is becoming aware of the Holy from
> the gut level, it is not yet completely conscious
> (can't be seen clearly). . . . Here Swedenborg is led
> to believe that he is being given something for his
> guidance. He doesn't sound entirely sure of this
> and indeed what he is being given is at the gut
> level and isn't fully conscious. The reader who
> knows of the Hindu *kundalini* may recognize what
> Swedenborg is dealing with. Kundalini is the spir-
> itual that can be induced to rise just as Sweden-
> borg describes it, "started from below in the body
> and went up to the head." There are Hindu spiri-
> tual exercises that induce this, and Swedenborg,
> with no knowledge of these practices, happens to
> be following them.[2]

And, indeed, Swedenborg continues to refer to "shudderings" and "holy shudderings" in his journal, as we see
in dreams numbers 228, 242, 282, and 285. I am convinced that Swedenborg had experiences in the category that I am labeling "kundalini" energy and that
they, for him as well as for me, were a piece of the spiritual journey.

Yet, again, it was not experiences that mattered to
Swedenborg, but rather the living of one's life.

As he writes in *True Christian Religion* 522:

> It is asked, How can man enter into this union?
> The reply is, that he cannot, unless to some extent
> he removes his evils by repentance. It is said that
> man must remove them, because this is not done

---

2. *Swedenborg's Journal of Dreams*, Van Dusen commentary, 127.

147

by the Lord directly, apart from man's cooperation; which is also fully shown in . . . [my explantion of] freedom of choice.

As I have made clear, I have been very much helped on my journey by New Age perspectives and by Christian mystics and commentators, especially St. Teresa of Avila and Evelyn Underhill. The Sufis, the Hindus, and the Buddhists have also played a role in my understanding of my spiritual path. But it is to Swedenborg that I turn most often for an integration of all of these perspectives.

Because I have had such a strong sense of encountering "being" within myself during moments of peace, it has been important to me to understand Swedenborg's concepts of *esse* and *existere*. These terms are often translated as "being" and "coming forth" or "substance" and "taking form." These two, he says, cannot exist without each other. "Where there is Esse (being) there is Existere (taking form); one is not possible apart from the other," he writes in *Divine Love and Wisdom* 14. Elsewhere, in *Arcana Coelestia* 2621, he states, "Every person and every thing has its being from conception, but its coming forth from birth; and thus as conception is prior to birth, so being is prior to coming forth." So perhaps what I feel in those moments is the love within my soul. Swedenborg also speaks of *esse* as life itself, which is Jehovah alone (*Arcana Coelestia* 1735) and refers to love as the *esse* of everyone's life (*Heaven and Hell* 14). This is certainly reflective of what I've felt within: pure love. In other places, he refers to divine love as *esse* and divine wisdom as *existere* (*Divine Love and Wisdom* 34). He sees love and wisdom as being connected just as substance and form are. Our very souls, he says, in their being are love and

148

wisdom, which come from the Lord (*Divine Love and Wisdom* 395).

I am particularly struck by this passage from *Divine Love and Wisdom* 48:

> Who that is capable of discerning the essential character of love cannot see this? For what is it to love self alone, instead of loving some one outside of self by whom one may be loved in return? Is not this separation rather than conjunction? Conjunction of love is by reciprocation; and there can be no reciprocation in self alone. If there is thought to be, it is from an imagined reciprocation in others. From this it is clear that Divine love must necessarily have being [*esse*] and have form [*existere*] in others whom it may love, and by whom it may be loved. For as there is such a need in all love, it must be to the fullest extent, that is, infinitely in love itself.

This seems to describe my experience. As I move deeper into conjunction, I seem to think less about loving myself and focus more on love of others.

I am also very moved by this passage from Swedenborg, found in *Apocalypse Explained* 997 (4):

> As innocence is the very being [*esse*] of all good, so peace is the very being of all delight from good. . . . Peace is happiness of heart and soul arising from the conjunction of the Lord, . . . when all conflict and combat of evil and falsity with good and truth has ceased.

I feel that Swedenborg understood and described the kind of peace I have been feeling.

It is probably a stretch to consider whether

Swedenborg's stages of regeneration could correspond to chakras, but I'd like to consider briefly a possible relationship. I find it intriguing that Swedenborg's initial development of his concept of regeneration involved six steps to the seventh or celestial level. In his explanation, the six steps correspond to the six days of creation, as he explains in *Arcana Coelestia* 6–12.[3]

The first day or stage of regeneration is a void. It includes both the state of infancy as well as the state immediately prior to regeneration. The second is one in which a distinction is made between those things that belong to the human and those to the Lord; those of the Lord are called "remains." The first two chakras involve working with survival, emotions, and identity—all related in their way to growth and maturity, to moving away from the "other" of the parent to the recognition of a separate personality. Swedenborg sees the third state as repentance, in which one is starting to do works of charity, but still thinks these noble urges emanate from the self. In the third chakra, one starts to define self-will and care of others. In Swedenborg's fourth state, the person "becomes affected with love, and illuminated by faith." The fourth chakra is by the heart and is the one that teaches love. Swedenborg's fifth state involves "discourses from faith." The fifth chakra is located at the throat and involves communication and self-expression. Swedenborg's sixth state occurs when the person acts from both faith and love and becomes a spiritual person who is called an "image." The sixth chakra is located in the middle of the forehead, an area sometimes called the

3. I am grateful to Nanci Adair of Portland, Maine, who has also noted a similarity between Swedenborg's seven stages of regeneration and the chakras and was willing to share her thoughts with me.

"third eye." Here one deals with imagination and openness. The seventh day in the Swedenborgian regeneration scheme is that of the celestial person (*Arcana Coelestia* 84). This is generally considered to be the chakra of spirituality and service.

Thus, for me, Swedenborg's seven stages of regeneration provide similar views of spiritual development as can be seen from the seven chakras.

Of all of Swedenborg's concepts that seemed useful to me in understanding my spiritual life, his approach to "charity" and "uses" is particularly relevant, the one that would correspond to the final stage of regeneration, the celestial person.

Charity is not, to Swedenborg, a traditional concept of doing good and kindly deeds for others; it is far more radical and demanding. William Woofenden, a Swedenborgian scholar, explains that "Swedenborg looks for an incarnation of the spirit of Christianity, whether in the individual life or in that of society. He finds it not enough to do the Christian thing. . . . What is wanted is an embodiment of the spirit of well doing."[4]

Living a life of charity as Swedenborg outlined it is an intentional process. We must begin by examining our own evils. We are all born into evils; and unless we acknowledge them, we risk not only repeating them but adding to them. In a modern psychological sense, we might say that we are all born into the interpersonal dynamics of our families and societies. Our parents pass along to us many of the prejudices, rigidities, and weaknesses of their own and of their parents. Even parents

---

4. William Woofenden, "Introduction" in Emanuel Swedenborg, *The Doctrine of Charity*, 2nd edition (West Chester, Penna.: Swedenborg Foundation, 1995), xvi–xvii.

who try very hard not to pass on certain dimensions of their own family dynamics find that, unconsciously, much more is taught to children than they realize. We all inherit this psychological baggage. Before we can do any effective good in the world, we have to acknowledge what it is that we have absorbed. We have to acknowledge it, confess it before the Lord, and be willing to change.

So the first step in charity is repentance. What is the second step? Swedenborg is clear: in *Charity* 14, he writes, "The second step in charity is to do good things for the reason that they are useful." This gets us back to the idea of conjunction. There is a conjunction of souls between my neighbor and myself. I am in you, you are in me, and we both reflect the Divine. How can I do evil to one with whom I live in union? It would be doing evil to myself.

Now, according to Swedenborg, my inner intention and my outer actions are in harmony.

There is a scale to determine who my neighbor is and which neighbor is worthy of my love: only the good and the true are our neighbors. The scale begins with the individual, but then moves to the community, the country, and the human race (*Charity* 72). A community is like a composite person. It is a neighbor to the extent to which it renders good service. The more it renders service, the more it is a neighbor.

My country is my neighbor according to its spiritual, moral, and civil good (*Charity* 83). Yet, I do not want to do anything that will strengthen my country in any evil or falsity (*Charity* 86). From this, we might conclude that there are times when I need to stand up to unjust laws or policies of my country because my neighbor, in the widest sense, is the entire human race.

At this point in the discussion of charity, Sweden-borg talks about "uses." Wilson Van Dusen describes "use" as "the fitting together of things, how each fits with and contributes to others. It is a way of looking at things that gets beyond the thing-in-itself to see how it fits into the whole."[5] This understanding of uses ties Swedenborgian theology to an ancient spiritual concept that has appeared in all cultures.

This brings us to a very significant dimension of Swedenborgian uses. One's daily occupation is an act of charity. Looking to the Lord and avoiding evils as sins, people who do the work of their office or employment "sincerely, justly, and faithfully" become embodiments of charity, Swedenborg writes in *Charity* 158. Our life's work—whatever it may be—is charity when done with the right attitude. We do not need to undertake a glam-orous and politically significant action to be in charity. Faithfully and mindfully doing one's life's work day in and day out is living a life of charity.

In viewing then, this trinity of love, wisdom, and uses, we can see various types of charitable actions. The first, and most important, is the daily fulfillment of my life's work when done after repentance and with love. Another type is that of doing good deeds for my neigh-bors, my community, my country, or the world.

Our ability to discern—our rationality—and our freedom to choose are what make us human, as opposed to the animals. We can think about things that facili-tate our being good neighbors to others and being in a good relationship with the Divine, or we can think

5. Wilson Van Dusen, "Uses: A Way of Personal and Spiritual Growth," in *The Country of Spirit: Selected Writings* (San Francisco: J. Appleseed & Co., 1992), 66.

about the opposite. We have that freedom. However, these abilities do not exist apart from the Lord. If we use our rationality and our freedom to open to higher levels, we will open ourselves to the higher levels of love and wisdom and we will become closer to God, according to Swedenborg.

The reason that Swedenborg is such a crucial spiritual mentor in my life has become clear to me. He, too, had a broad range of personal experiences. Some of them were clearly psychic experiences, such as his seeing a fire that was taking place miles away. Others were types of experiences that come from Christian mysticism, such as encounters with Christ. Others included energies and shudderings that sound similar to descriptions of the kundalini. He, too, engaged in spiritual disciplines involving meditation, breathing, prayer, scripture reading, and journal writing.

He could affirm all of these types of experiences others encountered before him and others have discovered long after him. Yet, unlike so many recipients of psychic and mystical encounters, he never placed importance on them for salvation. As so many others conclude, many of these experiences come from "grace." One does not choose them. Some who do practices for years to bring on such experiences never have them. Others with no background of spiritual practices are plunged into intense mystical experiences and psychic phenomena.

Swedenborg had such a grounded way of understanding his experiences, which has given me a framework for making sense of my own. Ultimately, all that matters is the "uses" of any experience. I know that, if my spiritual experiences do not give me great zest for living a life a charity, then they serve no purpose.

For Swedenborg, it is *living* the life of charity, rather

than having experiences, that leads to redemption. It is how we live life that brings us to God and redemption. God comes to us out of goodness of our living. Our freedom of choice is to live a good life and to respond to the Lord's presence in our lives. That is where I found free will. I do not choose how the Lord will come to me in my life, only how I will respond. I do not choose what spiritual experiences I will have, but I do choose how I will live out each day.

After years of struggle, I feel I have finally come to accept the mystical in my life, and to feel confident that it is now grounded in a context of living. It is important to me to work to change the world in the small ways I'm able to. It is important to me to be able to live each day as though it could my last opportunity to be a force for good in the world. Because it could be.

My mysticism leaves me convinced of the continuation of life after the death of the physical body. In gaining that certainty, I feel more than ever the importance of every moment of every day and that life is meant to be lived to the fullest.

155

QUESTIONS FOR
JOURNALING AND DISCUSSION

1. What dimensions of your daily life could be considered "uses" in the Swedenborgian sense?

2. Have you ever had any shaking, shuddering, rushes of energy, or other possible signs of kundalini energy? Do you know others who have experienced this? If so, what was your/their experience like? What role might it have played in spiritual development?

3. How would you characterize your spiritual path today? Your relationship to the Divine? What are the strengths of your spiritual life right now? What areas would you like to work on further? Where can you get support on your spiritual journey?

TOWARD A
SWEDENBORGIAN SPIRITUALITY

It was a warm evening in June 1998 as I sat around a
table with a dozen Sisters of Mercy at their facility in
Nashua, New Hampshire. Many of us had spent the past
couple of years in theological reflection groups on various topics, and I was asked to give an overview and sum-
mary of our work on world religions.

I shared some of the personal journey that you have
just read. I pointed out that my own mysticism and theological roots are Christian within a Swedenborgian
framework, but that I have turned to many other traditions to understand and amplify my journey, including
the Sufis, Buddhists, and Hindus. Roman Catholic nuns
of the past, in particular, St. Teresa, have been significant guideposts along the way for me.

As I shared this, I realized the depth of these truths

157

for me. I consider it crucial to be able to utilize a wide range of traditions to explore and understand my spirituality in the fullest sense possible. Yet, it is equally significant to me that I have a tradition to call home, which provides me with community and an anchor.

I see my own spiritual journey as the story of many in my generation. I am a baby-boomer, having been born in 1947 just after World War II. We are the generation that moved into the 1960s convinced that we knew more than any generation before us. We thought we knew how to end war—and ultimately we did play a big role in ending one. After a decade of political action, many of us drifted into the 1970s wondering "what next?" and looking at our spirituality. We were not impressed with mainstream Western religion, and the New Age emerged on the scene. We turned to Eastern traditions and integrated them with the opening of our psychic centers. We insisted on freedom of choice in spirituality and introduced the concept of the spiritual smorgasbord, where one could pick and choose from a variety of traditions.

This was the strength of the New Age of the 1970s and perhaps still is today: its openness to a wide number of traditions and its support of many Eastern traditions within a Western culture. Its weakness, however, is that it is not itself a religious tradition. The New Age movement does not have the grounding and generations of community that allow mysticism to flourish safely and deeply.

Because of this, some New Agers become seekers after phenomena and personal acclaim rather than travelers along the road of spiritual growth. There is also a tendency in some New Agers to emphasize private spiritual experience over action in the world. Of course, there are outstanding exceptions to this latter tendency; I think of David Spangler as an obvious one.

During my own years as an active participant in the New Age culture, I was confused about the difference between psychic phenomena and spiritual growth. At times, I saw the presence of psychic experiences, such as channeling, as evidence of spiritual advancement. I functioned within communities that saw *me* as a spiritual leader because of my channeling abilities and frequently urged me to tell people of their "past lives" and futures.

While such affirmation appealed to one side of me, it also brought me fear and anxiety, for I struggled with how one could assess the validity of channeled material and psychic experiences. I was not utilizing any of the traditional religious mystical paths. If I were, I would have heard that psychic experiences for some are a stage along the spiritual path, that they can be dangerous to the ego, that they should not be sought for their own sake, but rather just accepted with humility when they are present. Nor was I part of a tradition that could have warned me that they can be the first step of a spiritual journey that moves to a steep, rocky pathway, which many have called a dark night of the soul. When I found myself in a classic "dark night" (or as I prefer, wilderness wandering), I could find no explanation for why my psychic spirituality had come to an end. It was years later that I discovered the mystical traditions of the world and began to understand that the path I walked was an ancient one that many had been down before me.

My own life fell apart under the weight of psychic experiences that had no place to grow and develop, followed by years of wilderness wandering. I came to feel unable to provide spiritual leadership without a community of faith to support me, a theological tradition to help me discern truth from falsity, and peers to hold me accountable to standards of ethics.

I found those things for myself when I was drawn into the Christian mystical tradition, which solidified for me in the context of Emanuel Swedenborg's writings and the Swedenborgian Church. Community has allowed my mysticism to flourish by providing frameworks and traditions.

I consider myself a mystic because my beliefs come out of my heart and resonate with the experiences of spirit in my life. Traditionally, mysticism was seen as a rare form of spirituality that was largely confined to monasteries and other modes of isolated living, cut off from the larger society. Many writers on spirituality today—such as William Johnston, Harvey D. Egan, Llewelyn Vaughan-Lee, and Andrew Harvey—argue that mysticism is becoming a part of everyday life for ordinary people.

In particular, Andrew Harvey sees a modern form of enlightenment as one of passionate involvement in saving our planet and working to change the physical, political, and emotional life on the earth. He thinks that we don't need gurus to do this. In fact, gurus have tended to serve the institutions of power, keeping spiritual truths from women, homosexuals, the poor, and other oppressed members of society.

Harvey expands on his thoughts that we are entering a new era of enlightenment by saying, "Another way of looking at this era would be to see it as the era of the sacred marriage, the marriage between masculine and feminine, action and prayer, politics and mysticism."[1]

---

1. Catherine Ingram, "Teachers and Seekers: An Interview with Andrew Harvey," *Yoga Journal* (August 1995): 63.

This way of looking at mysticism is very Sweden-borgian. Swedenborg does not use the word "mystical" very often, but most of his references to it are quite positive. He uses it to describe the internal meaning of the Word. He also uses it to refer to the mystical union of "being one," as found in John 17: 21–23.

Yet, I think that the bulk of Swedenborg's theology is what I would call mystical. For he calls us to an active spirituality, where we must encounter the Lord within our hearts as well as in the public arena in which we live our lives. He calls us to move beyond concepts of dualism in all dimensions of our lives. He urges us to explore the oneness that unites all peoples, of different beliefs and races, into one humanity, pushing us to recognize the oneness of divinity and our union with that divinity.

What Swedenborg wrote was radical in the 1700s. These ideas are far more accepted today, in part because our spiritual understandings have become more sophisticated. They are also more accepted because science is coming to validate these concepts, particularly through the work of quantum physics. As physicist Michael Talbot says, "If Emanuel Swedenborg were alive today, it is very likely that he would consider many of the findings of the 'new physics' compatible with his own thought."[2] Perhaps many people around the world have learned to access the mode of reception more readily, and mysticism is entering everyday life in a way that was not known in the past.

I believe that my mystical story is not so much a

---

2. Michael Talbot, "Swedenborg and the Holographic Paradigm," in Robin Larsen, ed., *Emanuel Swedenborg: A Continuing Vision* (New York: Swedenborg Foundation, Inc., 1988), 442.

personal journey as a cultural one; I suspect that as a culture we are moving out of wilderness into a period of a new union with the Divine. The mystical experience of direct encounter with God is no longer for a handful of contemplatives in convents, monasteries, and temples far from the struggles of the world. Rather, as a society we are being called to encounter our mysticism—to find personal, intimate relationship with the Divine and to take all of ourselves, all of our being into that relationship. If God's influx is within each of us, then we relate to God as we encounter each other. Developing more loving connectedness with each other and our planet is another way of coming to know the Lord.

I see the energy of our times being transmuted into a new spirituality in which mysticism and active, loving lives will become the norm.

So, this is my attempt to define mysticism. It involves relating to the Divine in a way that is both transcendent and immanent. God is part of our very soul, and we walk through the mansions of our inner castles into a union with the Lord. God is also part of the humanity in every one of us, so whatever we do for the least of the creatures on earth we are doing for and to the Divine Spirit. I am not alone in this vision: many modern Christian theologians are developing a concept of encountering God through relationship with other human beings. The Divine calls us to action in the world. Both the inner experience of finding union in our interior mansions and the active work to manifest radical divine love on the earth are mysticism.

There are certainly pitfalls along the road of the mystical journey. One of them is that psychiatric issues can disguise themselves as mystical experience. Because of these pitfalls on the journey, I consider it essential that mysticism take place within the context of community. The feedback and support of community members are critical to keeping a mystic grounded. Other people are also needed to help the mystic continue to take her/his spirituality into the world, rather than try to live it in isolation.

There are many resources for community support. Virtually every religious tradition has a mystical strain with a rich literature and modern-day practitioners. Increasingly, mental health professionals and physicians are learning to recognize the signs of a person encountering a spiritual experience.[3]

I frequently turn to Swedenborg to help me define a healthy mysticism. Some of the main points I see him making are:

1. Keep your focus on regeneration.

2. Work at regeneration. The Lord will seek you out, and you can choose how to respond.

3. Avoid seeking spirit contact, as you can easily encounter evil spirits.

4. Engage in active work in the world. Find your "uses" within the larger society.

---

3. Regarding mental health issues, see *The Journal of Transpersonal Psychology*, which does outstanding work in exploring the differences between psychiatric conditions and mystical experiences. Also, the Spiritual Emergency Network (SEN) has representatives around the country who help people incorporate spiritual experience into their lives in a healthy manner.

5. Deepen your love of the Lord and your neighbors and be less concerned with gratification of your ego.[4]

In the final analysis, there are several points I wish to emphasize:

1. Mysticism is normal. It is a part of daily life and spirituality, rather than something separate from them. Everyone has had some experience of sensing of presence of a Higher Power. Many people describe having such a feeling occurring while listening to music, sitting on a beach, walking in the woods, watching a sunset, or even doing daily tasks such as washing dishes. The momentary sense of good will, peace, and serenity that can come to anyone at any time is, in my mind, an example of the grace of mysticism.

2. The mystical moment is one of grace. Ultimately, we don't choose a mystical moment of feeling oneness; it chooses us. However, prayer and meditation are particularly useful in helping develop the right frame of mind for letting the moment come. Allowing oneself to have times of relaxation and peace is very important; the hectic lives so many of us lead make it hard for the Divine to make itself known to us.

3. Mysticism is active rather than passive. It is seeking God in the heart and in connection with others.

---

4. I owe special thanks to Jun-chol Lee and Adam Seward, students at the Swedenborg School of Religion, who were enrolled in my class Pastoral Care II in the spring of 1998, for helping to develop Swedenborgian criteria for healthy mysticism, and to guest speaker Joann Lutz, LICSW, who helped us shape an understanding of these issues.

4. Mysticism is a journey, not an experience. The mystical path is a lifelong spiritual journey. There may be many experiences along the way, but they are not the core of mysticism.

5. The mystical journey is not taken on a straight path. Rather, it is more like a spiral. Ultimately, the best description of an unfolding journey may be one of moving between dualism and unity, of feeling separate from the source and of feeling as a part of the whole. As we walk along the spiritual path, it may be that the times of dualisms shorten and the periods of unity increase. Finding the pathway home gets easier and the journey back there happens more quickly.[5]

My hope in sharing my story is that you will be encouraged to share your story with someone in your life. Each of our stories is unique. Each of us has a spiritual journey to the center and a relationship with the Divine that defines the nature of that journey. I believe it is our human destiny to find our home and live at peace with the Divine. I believe it is our human calling to work to make the world and the planet a safer place for people to make their journeys.

I see us all being called into a mysticism for the twenty-first century; a mysticism of connection, where we can be together and love each other in community, communities that learn to respect diversity, to function without power abuses or oppression. I see a mysticism of transformation and transmutation.

---

5. I am particularly grateful for a workshop by Jerry Thomas, which helped me appreciate the concept of moving in and out of unity.

All of the religions traditions have something to share about the mystical journey. That includes us Swedenborgians, who have historically tended not to speak out about what our writings have to offer on living a spiritual life. We respect all paths to God, so do not speak much about ourselves, preferring to encourage others to follow their own traditions. But we also need to speak out and share who we are. I call upon my fellow Swedenborgians to share our journeys and our traditions with others.

I call upon all of the closet mystics out there—of whatever faith tradition, or of no faith tradition—to speak out so that we can share our stories with each other.

Finally, I call upon you, reading this material, to identify the crucial elements of your own story and find ways to share it. Let's begin talking openly with each other about our inner spirituality and supporting each other in going deeper within to find peace, as well as working to bring peace to a hurting world. Let's join hands and together discover what the mysticism of the future holds for us.

A SWEDENBORGIAN JOURNAL FOR THE SPIRITUAL JOURNEY

This journal is adapted from Emanuel Swedenborg's writings on the stages of regeneration or spiritual growth.

I invite you to reflect on the journey of your soul to find God. You are encouraged to think of your journey as one in which you move in and out of phases. You will find this journal of greatest benefit if you share your answers with others: a spiritual growth group, a spiritual mentor, a minister, or a special friend.

THE BEGINNING

1. Review your life from the earliest time you can remember.

   a. Look at all the ways you may have experienced a spirit outside yourself.
   b. Examine all that you were taught about God.

2. Consider your adult spiritual life.

   a. Did it have a clear beginning or did it continue from childhood?
   b. Write or talk about how it began or has continued.
   c. Was there any trauma or crisis that propelled you into the spiritual life?

GOD'S THINGS

1. Which things within you would you identify as coming from the Divine?

   a. Think of attributes of your personality, your feelings, your abilities, and your gifts.
   b. How could you use these aspects in your life now?

2. Which parts of yourself that were added by life to your divine aspects might need to be discarded on the spiritual journey?

REPENTANCE

1. What things from your past are mistakes or sins that you regret?

    a. Make a list of these regrets.

    b. With whom can you share this list to help you let go of your regrets?

2. Are there any things you need to do for others to make up for the past?

3. Are there changes you want to make in yourself to make it less likely that you will make the same mistakes again?

4. What things have been done to you that caused you hurt and pain?

    a. List those injuries.

    b. What do you need to do to move beyond the hurt and pain?

LOVE

1. What does "love" mean to you?

2. Who and what do you love?

3. Do you feel that you love the Divine?

4. Who loves you? Do you feel that God loves you? How do you experience that love?

FAITH

1. How would you describe your relationship with the Divine?

    a. Is there an image that comes to mind that would describe it?

    b. Can you draw or paint a picture of the relationship?

    c. Can you write a letter to God about how you see the relationship?

    d. How is the Divine making itself known in your life?

    e. Do you encourage or discourage this attention?

2. How would you like your relationship with the Divine to be different? What could you do to make it different?

3. How would you describe your faith and beliefs at this time?

CHARITY

1. Talk or write about your daily life.

    a. Where in a typical day do you have opportunities to do good for others?

    b. What do you do with these opportunities?

2. How do your daily activities contribute to the good of society?

3. What do you do to make the planet healthier?

4. Are there things you feel called to do for the planet, for society, for other individuals? What are they, and how would you integrate them into your life?

THE CELESTIAL PERSON

1. What do you do for yourself to take a break from your many activities? How do you relax and nurture your body?

2. What do you do to nurture your spirit? What spiritual disciplines do you observe in your life?

3. Where do you find spiritual community? Does this community meet your needs?

4. Do you have a spiritual director or mentor who helps you on your journey? If so, how is that relationship working? If you are dissatisfied, where could you search for a new mentor?

5. How do you integrate the active parts of your life and the times of quiet? Can you keep them in balance? If not, what is out of balance and how can you work with it?

BIBLIOGRAPHY

These are the materials I read or consulted in my attempts to understand my experiences. The ones I recommend for basic reading are marked with an asterisk.

Beer, Frances. *Women and Mystical Experience in the Middle Ages.* Rochester, N.Y.: University of Rochester Press, 1992.

Borg, Marcus J. *Meeting Jesus Again for the First Time: The Historical Jesus and the Heart of Contemporary Faith.* San Francisco: Harper, 1995. *

Bouyer, Louis. *Women Mystics: Hadewijch of Antwerp, Teresa of Avila, Therese of Lisieux, Elizabeth of the Trinity, Edith Stein.* Trans. Anne Englund Nash. San Francisco: Ignatius Press, 1993.

Bragdon, Emma. *The Call of Spiritual Emergency: From Personal Crisis to Personal Transformation.* San Francisco: Harper & Row, 1990. *

Braud, Ann. *Radical Spirits: Spiritualism and Women's Rights in Nineteenth-Century America.* Boston: Beacon Press, 1989.

Broughton, Rosemary. *Praying with Teresa of Avila.* Winona, Minn.: St. Mary's Press, 1990.*

Brueggemann, Walter. *Hopeful Imagination: Prophetic Voices in Exile.* Philadelphia: Fortress Press, 1986.

Bruyere, Rosalyn L. *Wheels of Light: Chakras, Auras, and*

the Healing Energy of the Body. New York: Simon & Schuster, 1994.

Capra, Fritjof. *The Tao of Physics.* New York: Shambhala Publications, 1976.*

———. *The Turning Point: Science, Society and Rising Culture.* New York: Simon & Schuster, 1982.*

Dole, George F., and Robert H. Kirven. *A Scientist Explores Spirit.* 2nd ed. West Chester, Penna.: Chrysalis Books, 1997.

Egan, Harvey D., S.J. *Christian Mysticism: The Future of a Tradition.* New York: Pueblo Publishing Co., 1984.

Eisler, Riane. *Sacred Pleasure: Sex, Myth, and the Politics of the Body.* San Francisco: Harper. 1995.*

Eller, Cynthia. *Living in the Lap of the Goddess: The Feminist Spirituality Movement in America.* New York: Crossroad, 1993.

Feuerstein, Georg. *Sacred Sexuality: Living the Vision of the Erotic Spirit.* New York: Putnam Publishing Group, 1992.

Foote, Catherine J. *Survivor Prayers: Talking with God about Childhood Sexual Abuse.* Louisville, Ky.: Westminster/John Knox Press, 1994.*

Fox, Matthew. *The Coming of the Cosmic Christ: The Healing of Mother Earth and the Birth of a Global Renaissance.* San Francisco: Harper and Row, 1988.*

Frawley, David. *Tantric Yoga and the Wisdom Goddesses: Spiritual Secrets of Ayurveda.* Salt Lake City, Utah: Passage Press, 1994.

Gately, Edwin. *A Mystical Heart: 52 Weeks in the Presence of God.* New York: Crossroad, 1998.

Giles, Mary, ed. *The Feminist Mystic and Other Essays on Women and Spirituality.* New York: Crossroad, 1982.*

Gilson, Anne Bathurst. *Eros Breaking Free: Interpreting*

173

Sexual Theo-Ethics. Cleveland, Ohio: Pilgrim Press, 1995.

Greenwell, Bonnie. *Energies of Transformation: A Guide to the Kundalini Process.* Saratoga, Calif.: Shakti River Press, 1995.

Gross, Shelley, ed. *The Mystic in Love: A Treasury of World Mystical Poetry.* New York: Bantam Books, 1976.*

Halligan, Fredrica R., and John J. Shea. "Beginning the Quest: Wither the Divine Fire?" in Fredrica R. Halligan and John J. Shea, eds., *The Fires of Desire: Erotic Energies and the Spiritual Quest.* New York, Crossroads, 1992.

Harvey, Andrew, and Mark Matousek. *Dialogues with a Modern Mystic.* Wheaton, Ill.: Quest, 1994.*

Heyward, Carter. *Our Passion for Justice: Images of Power, Sexuality, and Liberation.* New York: Pilgrim Press, 1984.*

————. *Touching Our Strength: The Erotic as Power and the Love of God.* San Francisco: Harper, 1989.

Hillman, James. *Archetypal Psychology: A Brief Account.* Dallas: Spring Publications, 1983.

————. *Loose Ends: Primary Papers in Archetypal Psychology.* Dallas: Spring Publications, 1975.

Hitchcock, John L. *Atoms, Snowflakes, and God: The Convergence of Science and Religion.* Wheaton, Ill.: Theosophical Publishing House, 1982.*

Houston, Jean. *Godseed: The Journey of Christ.* Wheaton, Ill.: Quest Books, 1992.*

————. *Public like a Frog: Entering the Lives of Three Great Americans.* Wheaton, Ill.: Quest Books, 1993.

————. *The Search for the Beloved: Journeys in Mythology*

and Sacred Psychology. New York: Jeremy P. Tarcher/Perigee Books, 1987.*

Irving, Darrel. *Serpent of Fire: A Modern View of Kundalini.* York Beach, Maine: Samuel Weiser, Inc., 1995.

Johari, Harish. *Chakras: Energy Centers of Transformation.* Rochester, Vt.: Destiny Books, 1987.

Johnson, Robert M. *Mind Frontiers: A Study of Transpersonal Psychology.* Southboro, Mass.: Awareness Center Press, 1991.

Johnston, William. *Christian Mysticism Today.* San Francisco: Harper & Row, 1984.*

Jordan, Judith V., et al. *Women's Growth in Connection: Writings from the Stone Center.* New York: The Guilford Press. 1991.*

Kavanaugh, Kieran, and Otilia Rodriguez. *The Collected Works of St. Teresa of Avila.* Three volumes. Washington, D. C.: ICS Publications, 1976.

Kornfield, Jack. *A Path with Heart: A Guide through the Perils and Promises of Spiritual Life.* New York: Bantam Books, 1993.*

Larsen, Robin, et al, eds. *Emanuel Swedenborg: A Continuing Vision: A Pictorial Biography and Anthology of Essays and Poetry.* New York: Swedenborg Foundation, Inc. 1988. *

Lawson, Carol S., ed. *Gold from Aspirin: Spiritual Views on Chaos and Order from Thirty Authors.* West Chester, Penna.: Swedenborg Foundation, 1995.*

LeShan, Lawrence. *The Medium, the Mystic, and the Physicist: Toward a General Theory of the Paranormal.* New York: Viking Press, 1974.*

Louth, Andrew. *The Origins of the Christian Mystical Tradition: From Plato to Denys.* Oxford, England: Clarendon Press, 1981.

175

Markus, Gilbert, ed. *The Radical Tradition: Revolutionary Saints in the Battle for Justice and Human Rights*. New York: Doubleday, 1993.

May, Gerald G. *Will and Spirit: A Contemplative Psychology*. San Francisco: Harper & Row, 1992.

McNamara, William. *Mystical Passion: The Art of Christian Loving*. Amity, N.Y.: Amity House, 1977.*

Milhaven, John Giles. *Hadewijch and Her Sisters: Other Ways of Loving and Knowing*. New York: State University of New York Press, 1993.*

Miller, Robert J., ed. *The Complete Gospels: Annotated Scholars Version*. San Francisco: Harper, 1994.

Mommaers, Paul, and Jan Van Bragt. *Mysticism Buddhist and Christian: Encounters with Jan van Ruusbroe*. New York: Crossroads, 1995.

Moody, Raymond, with Paul Perry. *Reunions: Visionary Encounters with Departed Loved Ones*. New York: Villiar Books, 1993.

Mookerjee, Ajit. *Kundalini: The Arousal of the Inner Energy*. Rochester, Vt.: Destiny Books, 1986.

Moore, Thomas, ed. *A Blue Fire: Selected Writings by James Hillman*. New York: Harper Perennial, 1989.*

———. *Care of the Soul: A Guide for Cultivating Depth and Sacredness in Everyday Life*. New York: Harper Perennial. 1994.*

———. *Meditations on the Monk Who Dwells in Daily Life*. New York: Harper/Collins. 1994.

Moore, Sebastian. *Let This Mind Be in You: The Quest for Identity through Oedipus to Christ*. Minneapolis, Minn.: Winston Press., 1985.

Muto, Susan. *John of the Cross for Today: The Dark Night*. Notre Dame, Ind.: Ave Maria Press, 1994.

Myss, Carolyn. *Anatomy of the Spirit: The Seven Stages of*

Power and Healing. New York: Three Rivers Press, 1996 .*

Nelson, James. *Embodiment: An Approach to Sexuality and Christian Theology*. Minneapolis, Minn.: Augsburg, 1978.

Nelson, James B. *Body Theology*. Louisville, Ky: Westminster/John Knox Press, 1992.

Petroff, Elizabeth Alvida. *Body and Soul: Essays on Medieval Woman and Mysticism*. New York: Oxford University Press, 1994.

Redfield, James, and Carol Adrienne. *The Celestine Prophecy: An Experiential Guide*. New York: Warner Books, 1995.

Roberts, Bernadette. *The Experience of No-Self: A Contemplative Journey*. Albany, N. Y.: State University of New York Press, 1993.

————. *The Path to No Self: Life at the Center*. Albany, N. Y.: State University of New York Press, 1985.

Sannella, Lee. *The Kundalini Experience: Psychosis or Transcendence?* Lower Lake, Calif.: Integral Publishing, 1992.

Shrady, Maria, trans. *Johannes Tauler Sermons*. New York: Paulist Press, 1985.

Sheldrake, Philip. *Spirituality and History: Questions of Interpretation and Method*. New York: Crossroads, 1992.

Sigstedt, Cyriel. *The Swedenborg Epic: The Life and Works of Emanuel Swedenborg*. London: Swedenborg Society, 1981.

Simsic, Wayne. *Praying with John of the Cross*. Winona, Minn.: St. Mary's Press, 1993.

Small, Jacquelyn. *Embodying Spirit: Coming Alive with Meaning and Purpose*. New York: Hazelden Books, 1994.*

177

Smith, Martin. *A Season for the Spirit.* Cambridge, Mass.: Cowley Publications, 1991.

———. *The Word Is Very Near You: A Guide to Praying with Scripture.* Cambridge, Mass.: Cowley Publications, 1989. *

Sovatsky, Stuart. *Eros, Consciousness and Kundalini: Deepening Sensuality through Tantric Celibacy and Spiritual Intimacy.* Rochester, Vt.: Park Street Books 1994.*

———. *Words from the Soul: Time, East/West Spirituality, and Psychotherapeutic Narrative.* Albany, N. Y.: State University of New York Press, 1998.*

Star, Jonathan, and Shahram Shiva, trans. *A Garden beyond Paradise: The Mystical Poetry of Rumi.* New York: Bantam books, 1992.

Stone, Barbara. *Cancer as Initiation: Surviving the Fire.* Chicago: Open Court, 1994.

Swedenborg, Emanuel. *Arcana Coelestia.* 12 vols. Trans. John Clowes. West Chester, Penna.: Swedenborg Foundation, 1994–1998.

———. *Divine Love and Wisdom.* Trans. George Dole. New York: Swedenborg Foundation, 1986. *

———. *The Doctrine of Charity.* Trans. John Whitehead. Revised by William R. Woofenden. West Chester, Penna.: Swedenborg Foundation, 1996. *

———. *Heaven and Hell.* Trans. George Dole. New York: Swedenborg Foundation, 1984.

———. *The True Christian Religion, Containing the Universal Theology of the New Church.* 2 vols. Trans. John C. Ager. West Chester, Penna.: Swedenborg Foundation, 1996.

Teresa of Avila. *The Interior Castle.* Translated and edited by Kieran Kavanaugh and Otillio Rodriguez. New York: Paulist Press, 1979.

————. *The Interior Castle by St. Teresa of Avila*. Edited and translated by E. Allison Peers. New York: Image Books, 1961.*

Thomas, Carolyn. *Will the Real God Please Stand Up: Healing Our Dysfunctional Images of God*. New York: Paulist Press, 1991.

Ulanov, Ann, and Barry Ulanov. *Primary Speech: A Psychology of Prayer*. Atlanta, Ga.: John Knox Press, 1982.

————. *Transforming Sexuality: The Archetypal World of Anima and Animus*. Boston: Sambhala, 1994.

Underhill, Evelyln. *Mysticism: The Preeminent Study in the Nature and Development of Spiritual Consciousness*. New York: Doubleday, 1990. *

Van Dusen, Wilson. *The Presence of Other Worlds: The Psychological/Spiritual Findings of Emanuel Swedenborg*. West Chester, Penna.: Chrysalis Books, 1994.*

Vaughan-Lee, Llewellyn. *The Bond with the Beloved: The Mystical Relationship between the Lover and the Beloved*. Inverness, Calif.: The Golden Sufi Center, 1993.*

————. *The Face before I Was Born: A Spiritual Autobiography*. Inverness, Calif.: The Golden Sufi Center, 1998.*

Wake, Wilma, *Wings and Roots: The New Age and Emanuel Swedenborg in Dialog*. San Francisco: J. Appleseed & Co., 1999.

————. [Sandra Gibson, pseud.] *Beyond the Body*. New York: Belmont-Tower Books, 1979.

————. [Sandra Gibson, pseud.] *Beyond the Mind*. New York: Tower Books, 1981.

Wiethaus, Ulrike. *Maps of Flesh and Light: The Religious Experience of Medieval Women Mystics*. Syracuse, N.Y.: Syracuse University Press, 1993.*

Wiseman, James A., trans. *John Ruusbroecc: The Spiritual Espousals and Other Works*. New York: Paulist Press, 1985.

Woods, Richard, ed. *Understanding Mysticism*. Garden City, N.Y.: Doubleday, 1980.